I dedicate this book to my parents for giving me a passion for literature and writing, the ability to think for myself, and an example of how to live out my Christian faith; to my husband for his belief in me and never-ending support; and to my children for introducing me to Harry Potter.

I also send special thanks to Dr. Barbara Lounsberry, Dr. Karen Tracey, Dr. John Swope, Dr. Julie Husband and Peter Rubie for their guidance in the early stages of this project.

A Parent's Guide to

Harry Potter

GINA BURKART

InterVarsity Press
Downers Grove, Illinois

InterVarsity Press
P.O. Box 1400, Downers Grove, IL 60515-1426
World Wide Web: www.ivpress.com
E-mail: mail@ivpress.com
©2005 by Gina Burkart

InterVarsity Press® is the book-publishing division of InterVarsity Christian Fellowship/USA®, a student movement active on campus at hundreds of universities, colleges and schools of nursing in the United States of America, and a member movement of the International Fellowship of Evangelical Students. For information about local and regional activities, write Public Relations Dept., InterVarsity Christian Fellowship/USA, 6400 Schroeder Rd., P.O. Box 7895, Madison, WI 53707-7895, or visit the IVCF website at <www.intervarsity.org>.

Design: Cindy Kiple

Images: tree with dark clouds: Tyler Gourey/Getty Images
        boy with book: Digital Vision/Getty Images

ISBN 0-8308-3288-2

Printed in the United States of America ∞

Library of Congress Cataloging-in-Publication Data

Burkart, Gina, 1971-
 A parent's guide to Harry Potter / Gina Burkart.
    p. cm.
 Includes bibliographical references.
 ISBN 0-8308-3288-2 (pbk.: alk. paper)
 1. Rowling, J. K.—Characters—Harry Potter—Handbooks, manuals,
 etc. 2. Potter, Harry (Fictitious character)—Handbooks, manuals,
 etc. 3. Children—Books and reading—Handbooks, manuals, etc. 4.
 Children's stories, English—Handbooks, manuals, etc. 5. Fantasy
 fiction, English—Handbooks, manuals, etc. 6. Wizards in
 literature—Handbooks, manuals, etc. 7. Magic in
 literature—Handbooks, manuals, etc. I. Title.
 PR6068.O93Z564 2005
 823'.914—dc22

                                                          2005004488

| P | 18 | 17 | 16 | 15 | 14 | 13 | 12 | 11 | 10 | 9 | 8 | 7 | 6 | 5 | 4 | 3 | 2 | 1 |
| Y | 20 | 19 | 18 | 17 | 16 | 15 | 14 | 13 | 12 | 11 | 10 | 09 | 08 | 07 | 06 | 05 |

CONTENTS

FOREWORD

This book is long overdue. It was detoured by fears about the Harry Potter books, and parents and Christian publishers needed to deal with the initial controversy and frightening predictions that the Harry Potter books would lead kids "directly into the occult." I was privileged to be able to help address those issues in my books. However, now that the controversy has subsided, we can focus on the positive aspects of these stories that kids and adults love so much. Truth be told, this is a book I would like to have written, but I am delighted to see that Gina Burkart has teamed up with InterVarsity Press to fill this need.

Gina has delivered a book that will help you delve into valuable themes within the stories so that you can have a wonderful shared learning experience as a family. I find Gina to be genuine in her faith in Jesus Christ, intelligent, articulate, well versed in both the Bible and Harry Potter, and—most memorably—passionate about passing on good values to her own children. I find in her a kindred spirit.

What she shares in this volume can be a springboard into a rich ongoing conversation with your children in which you can instill biblical values in ways that are enjoyable, extremely relevant to their daily challenges and interesting. She identifies a wealth of issues to discuss with your children in a thrilling and delightful shared literary experience. And she makes the conversation so easy.

Among the notable issues for families to discuss are friendship, family, self-sacrifice, temptations and the dangers of giving in, courage, the power of love, facing fears, the deepest desires of our hearts, growing up, bullying, protecting the innocent, dealing with injustice, helping those who are enslaved, racial bigotry, class snobbery, international cooperation, life and death, hatred, torture, tyranny, and terrorism—all relevant issues in today's world. By taking these issues on with our kids in a fantasy story, we help them face the challenges of our real world with confidence and parental guidance—which is necessary as children read the Harry Potter books. I commend you for taking this on with your children and on your children's behalf.

Now that the time for this excellent book has finally come, don't wait another minute before getting into it with your children. God bless you as you grow together through the shared literary and spiritual experience.

Connie Neal
Author of *What's a Christian to Do with Harry Potter?* and *The Gospel According to Harry Potter*

INTRODUCTION

The idea for this book came to me while I was reading *Harry Potter and the Sorcerer's Stone* with my children. I was intrigued and delighted with the Christian parallels that ran through the book, as well as the variety of pertinent issues they explored. My children often picked up on them as we engaged in some powerful discussions. These discussions challenged us to grow in faith and think critically about the world around us.

I also discovered that the books provided a special opportunity for my children and me to bond. These weren't the usual "How was your day?" discussions—not that those are bad. We had found a common and entertaining meeting ground. While I facilitated and led the discussions, we all partook enthusiastically and equally. I shared with and learned from them just as much as they shared with and learned from me. Our relationship deepened to a new level—and it continues to grow, in Harry Potter discussions and elsewhere.

As I enjoyed the richness and fun of our discussions while sharing the Harry Potter books, it occurred to me that perhaps other parents and educators could use the Harry Potter books in similar ways.

This book is broken into two parts. In part one the Harry Potter chronicles are compared to the fairy tale genre. Suggestions are given for using the Harry Potter books to foster moral growth and build relationships in which children can talk about the difficult issues and situations they face each day.

Part two unpacks and explores some of the themes that run

through the books. Practical questions and examples are provided to get you started talking about the many kid-relevant issues present in the books.

Children need to know that they can talk to caring and loving adults who will guide them and support them. Adults sometimes need to see life in new ways through the eyes of a child. The Harry Potter books provide opportunities for both. The goal of this book is to bring adults and children together as they grow in their Christian faith.

PART 1

WHAT CHILDREN CAN LEARN
FROM HARRY POTTER

1

THE HARRY HYPE

Children should be brought up in such a way that they
will fall in love with virtue and hate vice.

PLATO

In 1997 J. K. Rowling introduced us to Harry Potter with her brainstorm *Harry Potter and the Sorcerer's Stone* (called *Harry Potter and the Philosopher's Stone* in the United Kingdom). Since then, educators and parents alike have struggled with what to do with Harry Potter. Does he have a place in your home? in your classroom? How about the Christian classroom? Get to know Harry, and you will find the answer is yes!

Children love Harry because he conquers struggles they face daily, and he does so in a world of fantasy that appeals to their already active imagination. Harry is picked on by bullies, is treated unfairly at home, struggles with homework, forms friendships, makes mistakes and chooses between right and wrong. But more important, he shows how a weak child becomes strong and respected. His is the classic tale of how the weak become strong.

Harry enters a magical school where he gains fame, becomes the team hero in Quidditch matches, and wins battles with a troll, Professor Quirrell and Lord Voldemort. Children can't get enough. We are suddenly facing the problem of getting children's noses out of books rather than into them. "Since the Potter novels have been on the market, paperback sales of children's books increased by 24 percent totaling $660 million, and hardcover sales expanded by 11 percent totaling $1.6 billion. Books whose sales have significantly increased include C. S. Lewis' *The Chronicles of Narnia* series and Lloyd Alexander's 'The Black Cauldron Series.'"[1] Harry has convinced children to read. So why isn't he being showered with praise and awards?

Harry's creator, Rowling, *is* winning wide acclaim for Harry Potter. In fact, she has obtained a long list of awards since Harry was introduced in 1997: British Book Awards Children's Book of the Year, the Smarties Prize, *Publishers Weekly* Best Book of 1998, *School Library Journal* Best Book of 1998 and the Parenting Book of the Year Award that same year. Also, the Harry Potter books were the first children's books to claim spots on the *New York Times* bestseller lists since E. B. White's *Charlotte's Web* in the 1950s. And the books remained on the bestseller lists longer than many adult novels—creating another controversy.[2]

WORRIED ABOUT HARRY

Despite these impressive achievements, some adults are concerned that the Harry Potter books will have negative effects on our children. The worst-case scenario in circulation is that the Harry Potter series is a ploy of Satan to destroy our children. Proponents of this theory are appalled by the use of witchcraft to fight evil in the books. "The Truth About Harry Potter" on Freedomvillageusa.com states:

> Harry is a bonafide wizard and is being taught divination (crystal ball, and tealeaf reading) and other occult practices. He is

the hero and uses his powers of darkness to fight a greater power in the dark world (the evil Lord Voldemort) who murdered his mother (a witch) and his father (a wizard). This is saying that it's OK to use evil to fight evil if your intent is for self-gain. That is a cardinal doctrine of Satanism and will lead you to believe that you can control the use of evil.[3]

Some proponents of this position even believe the Harry Potter series is a recruitment tool for Wicca, witchcraft and the occult. They believe parents' and teachers' acceptance of these books leads children to believe that the occult and witchcraft are acceptable, legitimate arenas. Some anti-Harry folks say that the lightning bolt on Harry's forehead is a satanic symbol.

Proponents of these views feel so strongly that they have pushed to ban Harry Potter from school classrooms and libraries. The American Library Association has recorded another first for Harry Potter: there were more demands for these books' removal from classrooms, school libraries and reading lists than any other book in 1999. They cite a total of thirteen states challenging the Harry Potter books.[4] This has necessitated careful reviews of the First Amendment. In Wichita Falls, Texas, a federal judge ruled against a local law allowing controversial books to be pulled from library shelves. The law was found to be unconstitutional, as it violated the First Amendment.[5]

WHAT TO DO WITH HARRY

So what do we do about Harry? He has captured children's hearts, and the First Amendment protects him. He is here to stay. Yes, as some of the opponents have pointed out, there are areas of concern in the books—in particular Rowling's use of witchcraft and violence. But banning the books will only push children to read them in private without us, and the taboo areas will become the most attractive features of the books.

The best solution is to continue to be good educators and parents. We need to read the books with children—savor the stories, help them sort out the fantasy and reality, and discuss the serious issues that are presented.

When enjoyed in the classroom and at home, as well as used to discuss moral issues in the real world, the Harry Potter books can become powerful resources for training our children in critical thinking. They provide opportunities for parents and educators to take up real-life issues with children: child abuse, lying, friendship, dealing with bullies, death, and good and evil, to name a few. Reading not only becomes fun, but it connects children with adults and helps form powerful and meaningful relationships. Children and adults can use the Harry Potter books as springboards for discussion that allows them to understand each other and bond.

Nationally known storyteller, lecturer, author and language arts consultant Carol Hurst reinforces this point. Hurst explains that to fully acquire literacy, children need to engage in a dialogue with adults when they read. She says, "Books can no longer be taken in isolation. Bridges can and should be made by books. At first those bridges must be built by adults, but increasingly such bridges come from the children."[6]

MAKING CONNECTIONS

Harry Potter provides an excellent opportunity to build those bridges. But don't forget, these books should first and foremost be enjoyed. Rowling draws us into the classic battle of good versus evil in an imaginative and fun fantasy world. We make friends with Harry, Hermione and Ron. We take potions class from Snape and sneak through the woods to visit Hagrid in his Hut. We are tempted to join forces with Voldemort to gain fame and glory. With Harry, we choose good over evil and win!

All of these exciting adventures provide fertile ground for moral discussion. The theme of the Harry Potter books helps us to connect with C. S. Lewis's classic *The Lion, the Witch and the Wardrobe,* which Rowling has noted was one of her favorite childhood stories.

In *The Lion, the Witch and the Wardrobe*, four children—Peter, Susan, Lucy and Edmund—enter the magical land of Narnia, where numerous battles and adventures lead the children to a deeper understanding of themselves and the moral world. We especially see this through the character of Edmund, who betrays his siblings out of greed and a desire for power but later repents and fights beside them to destroy the White Witch. But the real Christian allegory occurs with Aslan the Lion. He is killed by the evil White Witch yet rises from death and thus becomes a Christ figure in the story.

Aslan parallels Christ, who was crucified and then resurrected to conquer death. After Aslan's resurrection, he explains to Susan and Lucy that

> though the Witch knew the Deep Magic, there is a magic deeper still which she did not know. Her knowledge goes back only to the dawn of time. But if she could have looked a little further back, into the stillness and the darkness before Time dawned, she would have read that when a willing victim who committed no treachery was killed in a traitor's stead, the Table would crack and Death itself would start working backward.[7]

We find a similar Christian parallel in *Harry Potter and the Sorcerer's Stone.* Though Harry's parents were killed in their battle with Lord Voldemort, Harry was saved by the love of his parents, particularly of his mother. This reminds us of Christ's loving sacrifice: he died on the cross so that humanity might live. In a heart-to-heart conversation with Harry, Professor Dumbledore explains:

> Your mother died to save you. If there is one thing Voldemort cannot understand, it is love. He didn't realize that love as powerful as your mother's for you leaves its own mark. Not a scar, no visible sign . . . to have been loved so deeply, even though the person who loved us is gone, will give us some protection forever. It is in your very skin. Quirrell, full of hatred, greed, and ambition, sharing his soul with Voldemort, could not touch you for this reason. It was agony to touch a person marked by something so good.[8]

The fantasy world of magic has been used for many years to teach children about the nature of good and evil. Other well-known stories such as *A Wrinkle in Time* by Madeline L'Engle and the Star Wars films by George Lucas also use fantasy to present themes of good versus evil. There are differences, of course, in the characters and settings. In *A Wrinkle in Time,* children travel through time and space to battle the Black Thing. In Star *Wars* Luke Skywalker and Obi Wan Kenobi use the force to battle Darth Vader.

Our imaginative minds are attracted to moral issues when they are given shape in a world of fantasy and magic. Creative authors take advantage of this and lure our minds into mystical realms of good and evil. Returning to reality, the reader is better equipped to recognize themes of good and evil in the real world.

Talking about these books in various settings allows us to make our jump back to reality with others. We share the fun of the story with others; we also clarify our thoughts and internalize the story's lessons. Just as Harry relies on Dumbledore at the end of each adventure to make sense of what has transpired, we can rely on each other to make sense of the stories and talk about the lessons we learned. As parents and educators, we often need to be Dumbledore for children. And as Harry teaches Dumbledore at times, children will also teach us.

Fantasy creators like Lucas, Lewis and Rowling get children excited about reading. We need to channel that excitement with discussions that bring us together and help us unravel what is really going on in Narnia, at Hogwarts and in the universe. Most important, we need to return to reality and apply the lessons of Hogwarts and Narnia to the real world. These are fictional places with fictional characters, but the issues they address are real. We need to bridge the gap. And as we do so, we have the chance to find our own imagination.

QUESTIONS TO BRIDGE THE GAP

- **What do you like best about Hogwarts? What do you like least? Why?**

- **Why do you think Dudley and Malfoy are so mean? How do you deal with people who act like Malfoy and Dudley?**

SPIRITUAL CONNECTIONS

Finding our imagination helps us grow spiritually. Many biblical teachings involve the battle of good versus evil. And some of them require us to stretch beyond what can be verified and proved with facts and evidence.

Children readily cross the boundaries of the ordinary in their thinking. Their attraction to the extraordinary helps them quickly bypass what can sometimes be an obstacle to faith for adults. Children move beyond the how and allow themselves to become enthralled and excited by the story.

We can catch their energy and help them to decipher the morals and lessons presented in the Bible. For example, in the Genesis account of creation, Adam and Eve battle Satan in the form of a snake while they live a garden life that involves no pain, no toil and no clothes. Satan is evil, and God is good. Adam and Eve lost the battle because they didn't obey God. They were overcome by greed and lust for power. They wanted to be more powerful than God.

Most children love this story. They rarely question how Satan can become a snake or doubt that a place such as the Garden of Eden existed. They dream of such a place. They believe God's Word and extract God's lessons with our help.

These lessons, often echoed in fantasy stories, are easy for many children to connect and relate to. The battle of good and evil is everywhere; it is part of life. Every new tale gives us a chance to take children back to the Bible, where it all began and is true.

In *Harry Potter and the Sorcerer's Stone,* Voldemort takes the shape of a snake, and Harry must do battle with him. Harry is tempted with power by Voldemort, as Eve was tempted by Satan. If Harry gives Voldemort the stone, Voldemort promises to share his power and eternal life with him. But unlike Adam and Eve, Harry doesn't yield to the temptation. Harry fights the snake and wins. Of course, Harry must battle Voldemort many more times. New struggles and temptations continue to arise for Harry, just as they do for us.

Relating our spiritual battles to Harry Potter empowers our children. As Jesus overcame Satan's temptations, we can say no to temptation. Children *can* overcome evil. Children *can* defeat Satan.

2

MORE THAN A STORY

Jesus' invitation to enter his kingdom comes in the form
of parables, a characteristic feature of his teaching.
. . . The parables are like mirrors for man.

CATECHISM OF THE CATHOLIC CHURCH 546

The beauty of literature is that it is never the same. When I reread stories from my childhood, I read them through new eyes. I bring new experiences to the stories and thus find new discoveries and meanings. Stories change as we change. And my children often notice things that I don't. We read the stories through a pair of bifocals, as our discussions reveal who we are and what we are struggling with. I learn to once again see life through the eyes of a child, and my children get a glimpse into the world of an adult. Together we grow in spirituality, faith, morality and love. We learn to accept and believe in a God that we can't see, taste, touch or smell. We look forward to an eternal life that will follow.

I spend much of my day in storyland with my children. During the summer, we read together in the afternoon and at bedtime. While roadtripping, I often read while my husband drives.

As I write this chapter, we are rereading *Harry Potter and the Prisoner of Azkaban,* since we just saw the movie. This makes travel go very fast, and it provides an excellent opportunity for us to bond as a family. We often stop in the middle of the story to discuss an issue or make a comment. It is also fun to point out how we see the book differently from the way the director of the movie did. For example, we all thought the movie's werewolf looks more like a hairless dog. And we really wished the director had shown throughout the movie how Hermione is using the hourglass to take more classes. Our favorite part was when Harry is riding Buckbeak. Discussion such as this not only brings us closer together and helps us understand one another but also fosters critical thinking.

Sharing stories like Harry Potter in the van has led to a practice of telling our personal stories there as well. We gather in the van frequently—before and after school, on the way to games and practices, before and after church. Sometimes our minivan becomes a confessional; other times it is the amphitheater of a children's dramatic production. Most often it is a meeting place where stories and secrets are shared and swapped.

Some of the craziest and most challenging moments of my day occur in that van, of course, but it also is the place where I get to hear (often in three different versions) what happened during the school day or in athletic practice. This is my time to listen, offer advice, guide and turn stories into teachable moments. Frequently I find myself using Bible stories, children's fairy tales and personal experiences as resources. Harry Potter is our favorite and most frequent meeting place.

Some of the recurring themes involve unfair punishment and instances of injustice in the classroom and on the playground. Stories speak volumes at these moments because they often combine children's emotions and logic. Children can relate to Harry Potter when he is unfairly punished by Professor Snape. They remember how

Cinderella felt when she was teased by her stepsister. They find relief when they hear that Mom also had to move her desk out into the hall for talking in class. They receive hope and encouragement in the knowledge that others have experienced what they have. They learn to relate to others, assess others' reactions to similar situations and, with guidance, choose a responsible and moral reaction to their situation. Additionally, they learn to trust and respect their parents as guardians and educators.

Claudia Royal comments that stories "teach truth in concrete form."[1] She notes that stories "open the windows" of their imagination, which allows them to "enter into the experience of others." This allows children to see outside their own lives. By allowing them to feel the intense emotions and situations of others in stories, we can "teach honesty, fair play, respect for custom and authority, love for parents, industry, and bravery."[2]

My son, like many children, does not get overly enthused about school. Math is his least favorite subject. He particularly struggles when he has a substitute or student teacher. So I wasn't particularly surprised when he came home last semester with a note from the student teacher saying that things had not gone well during math class. He had not been disrespectful; he was just unresponsive. He was very upset about the note and the situation. He believed he was being picked on.

Professor Snape and his Potions class provided a perfect example for exploring the situation and finding a solution. It also helped ease the tension and anxiety. We shared a few laughs and explored options for improving the situation.

Harry doesn't like Potions class because he often messes up in potions and feels incapable. Harry is also distrustful of Professor Snape. My son feels anxious and frustrated in math, and he is distrustful of new teachers. Discussing the story helped me understand how he felt. While his student teacher did not treat my son the way Professor Snape treats Harry, that was how my son perceived the situation. We compared Harry's situation with his. The teacher was not verbally abusing my son nor treating him unfairly. She was just trying to draw him into class activities. But my son felt picked on and singled out.

As he realized why he was feeling the way he was, he began to understand his unresponsive reaction. He was also able to understand why the teacher may have been frustrated. We arranged for a meeting. There was a lot less tension once my son and the teacher understood each other and arrived at an understanding. Things were not perfect, but they were better. Harry Potter had provided us with a starting point for resolving the issue. This is the power of a shared story!

Some of the most powerful stories come from our own life. And our lives are full of times when we have messed up or made a poor choice. I often tell such stories to my children when they are in the midst of punishment for one of their mistakes. They find reassurance in knowing that Mom, Dad or another respected adult also messed up. They also see that they can grow and get beyond it. Harry Potter often provides opportunities for my husband and me to share an experience of our own, which then often prompts our children to tell their stories.

In *How to Raise a Moral Child: The Moral Intelligence of Children,* Robert Coles explores why "someone else's memories often trigger our own."[3] I often relate to Hermione. I loved school and always had my hand up in class. I can now see how I probably annoyed my classmates. My son often relates to Harry, since he is less than enthusiastic about homework and assignments. But he loves sports, particularly baseball, just as Harry loves Quidditch. While Harry finds his confidence on his broom catching the Golden Snitch, my son finds his confidence on the pitching mound. My oldest daughter shares Hermione's inquisitive nature and love for solving a mystery, while my youngest daughter can relate to Ginny's struggles of being the youngest.

Stories can also be used to enhance and add intrigue to ordinary experiences. The theme of my daughter's summer camp this year was Harry Potter. She and her friend had their bags packed with Harry Potter stuff for weeks ahead of time. The fact that it was Harry Potter camp made it much more exciting. They imagined themselves going to Hogwarts. Our car became the Hogwarts Express.

At camp, they enjoyed being sorted by an old pail instead of a hat, worried about getting howlers, listened to readings out of all the Harry Potter books by the campfire, earned house points and had a Jell-O battle for the house cup. Luckily, they avoided the womping willow.

A MORAL COMPASS

Stories are also helpful in teaching morality. Stories help us make sense of our struggles. They help us understand that we play the biggest role in our own life. Likewise, they give us a context to understand our role. Stories offer meaning and reassurance.[4] They help us parents construct a moral compass for our children, because "stories also help us make sense of morality. How well do motives for virtuous behavior hold up without the sense that there is something like a plot to our lives? Not well at all. . . . But to feel that one has been given a role to play in a meaningful story . . . that is considerable motivation."[5]

William Bennett discusses this subject in the introduction to his *Books That Build Character.* He finds literature fertile ground for the planting of moral seeds. Furthermore, he argues that reading stories makes a person "morally literate" and thus better equipped to make an ethical decision when faced with a tough situation.[6]

We face an exciting and rewarding challenge—to raise moral children who care and want to make a difference in this world. We also have the task of playing and having fun with children. Combining these responsibilities allows us to pass on valuable gifts to our children—especially an internal moral compass to help them find their way through life's toughest and darkest forests.

3

THE MODERN FAIRY TALE

I don't think there's anyone in this room who grew up without fairies, magic and angels in their imaginary world. They aren't bad. They aren't serving as a banner for an anti-Christian ideology. If I have understood well the intentions of Harry Potter's author, they help children to see the difference between good and evil. And she is very clear on this.

REV. DON PETER FLEETWOOD, VATICAN NEWS CONFERENCE

Once upon a time children were taught moral lessons from fairy tales. The phrase "once upon a time" beckoned children to begin a journey of enchantment that would whisk them off to a location far away where they would encounter mystery, magic, pain and amusement. They would meet fairies, witches, villains and friends. By the time they returned, they would be refreshed with a new outlook on life and their everyday struggles. They would have a renewed faith in themselves and a better understanding of life and what it means to be human. The fairy tale was not just an escape or retreat but a moral compass for life.

But somewhere down the road, parents and educators became concerned about the influence of fantasy on young children's minds.

They feared fantasy would lead children away to never-never land and they would not return. Reality and fact were emphasized in education, and imagination was discouraged.

In our technological era, scientists strive to explain the mysteries of the universe. Computers have become common in the household and have made many human jobs obsolete. Cloning, the Internet and nuclear power shadow our discussions. And the education of children aims to equip them to succeed in such a world.

But what are children being taught about human relationships and the meaning of life? They may know what a human being is, but do they know how to form a meaningful relationship with one? Should they? Today success is not measured by relationships. In fact, relationships get in the way of a climb to the top of the corporate ladder. Anyway, when they are ready for a relationship, they can learn all they need to know from peers as they decide whether to pursue love or money. Right?

Having excised morality, religion and imagination from education, we ask in alarm, "What is wrong with our children?" The tragedy at Columbine shocked and stunned us as we saw and heard students open fire on teachers and fellow classmates. "Why are our children killing each other?" we asked. Almost daily, the news informs us of school violence, drug and alcohol abuse, delinquency, rebellion, sexual disease and teen pregnancy.

With our emphasis on fact and discouraging of imagination, perhaps our children never learned to value life. When we extracted the supernatural and morality from education, did we miss opportunities to help our children gain a sense for the meaning of life? We gave our children reality, but did we give them a means for understanding it? Children need a model for coping with and understanding reality.[1]

THE VALUE OF FAIRY TALES

Bruno Bettelheim, an educator and therapist of severely disturbed children, found two things imperative in helping children find meaning in their lives: parents (guardians) and literature.[2] The relationships of the parents (guardians) with the children and the transmission of cultural heritage through fairy tales give meaning to children's lives. These stories speak to children on their own emotional and psychological level. Fairy tales uncover children's repressed and hidden fears and bring them to the surface for understanding and healing. The stories offer images of the struggles life often throws at us and provide opportunities for finding both temporary and permanent solutions.[3]

Bettelheim found the fairy tale ideal literature for moral instruction because it offers "access to deeper meaning" and is able to reach children at their stage of moral development. The fairy tale holds children's attention, entertains and arouses curiosity, and enriches life by stimulating the imagination. The fairy tale develops intellect, clarifies emotions, is attuned to childhood anxieties and aspirations, gives recognition to childhood difficulties, and offers solutions to life challenges and problems.[4]

FEAR FACTOR

The fairy tale passes on lessons of heritage and life in the context of a fantasy world. It takes up the fundamental issues of good and evil, life and death, and recounts tasks and journeys that symbolize life.

Fairy tales also often contain terrifying and frightening scenes, which we object to and strive to protect children from. For example, Hansel and Gretel face a witch who wants to eat them, Cinderella is locked up by a wicked stepmother, and Little Red Riding Hood is pursued by a hungry wolf. But these frightening scenes allow children to feel a human emotion—fear—within the security of community and family. They allow the subconscious fears of children to surface and be released. Hansel and Gretel ultimately deal with the loss of their parents successfully (as does Harry Potter). Loss of parents is one of the greatest fears of children, yet it is often unspoken and hidden, thus causing anxiety.

The fairy tale allows children to face and deal with their fears. Donald Baker finds the frightening scenes of fairy tales necessary and therapeutic, as they release repressed fears and anxieties and demonstrate the need to respect others. Fairy tales allow children to confront their subconscious nightmares in a loving, secure setting. Reading these stories with children helps us understand their struggles, fears and anxieties. It allows us to offer a release for their terrors, guidance in understanding them, and support and reassurance as they seek a solution. As Baker eloquently claims, "Without the fairy tale we should never achieve any kind of humanity."[5]

Our instincts tell us to protect children. Naturally, we want to shelter them from scary situations such as those set up in fairy tales. We fear that the stories will traumatize them or at least bring nightmares and discomfort. But the main goal of the fairy tale is not to provoke fear. The fear is only a component of the story. The fairy tale is meant to "depict processes of development and maturation."[6] Those processes of development and maturation involve risks, journeys and tasks, some involving danger and naturally evoking fear. Allowing children to embark on these journeys with our support fosters healthy growth, maturation and development.

Harry Potter pictures a number of such journeys. Remember when Harry and Ron face Aragog in *Harry Potter and the Chamber of Secrets?* Aragog is described as "a spider the size of a small elephant," with "gray in the black of his body and legs, and each of the eyes on his ugly, pincered head was milky white."[7] Many children jump at the sight of a daddy longlegs. This scene forces us to face and release our fear with Harry and Ron when Aragog refuses to deny "fresh meat" to his tribe of spiders. With Harry and Ron, we find ourselves facing "a wall of spiders, clicking, their many eyes gleaming in their ugly black heads,"[8] eager to eat us. Luckily, Mr. Weasley's car comes to the rescue. This scene provides us with a perfect opportunity for discussing and releasing our fears of spiders.

QUESTIONS TO BRIDGE THE GAP

- **What does Harry battle that is scary?**

- **What is scary about those battles?**

- **Which is the scariest Harry Potter book?**

- **Why is that the scariest?**

- **How would you feel if you were Harry? Why?**

- **When have you felt that way?**

- **What can you do when you are afraid?**

- **What are your biggest fears? How do you deal with them?**

Some of the other journeys are more complex and reveal more philosophical truths. In the final battle of each book, Harry comes face to face with death and emerges victorious. At the end of each final battle, Professor Dumbledore helps Harry understand the journey and battle he has just undergone. This is an essential component of the story. Like the fairy tale, it reflects the journey of development and maturation.

As Harry succeeds in each battle, he gains more self-confidence and a fuller understanding of the battle of good and evil. In *Harry Potter and the Sorcerer's Stone,* only after the final battle with Lord Voldermort does Harry understand that it was the love of his mother that saved him. Professor Dumbledore tells him that evil could not touch something that is "so good." As with the fairy tale, here the terror of the final battle leads to a moral understanding of good and evil—and thus a better understanding of the meaning of life, rooted in Christ's sacrifice of love to overcome evil.

Connecting Harry Potter with the Christian faith perhaps best addresses our questions and concerns about the frightening nature of the Harry Potter story. For the Bible also contains many frightening accounts—and perhaps more so because they are true—that teach our children about morality, the meaning of life and God's power to save. Remember, Bettelheim argues that an experience of fear in the fantasy world is cathartic and therapeutic for children. It allows children to come back to reality refreshed and with a better understanding of how to deal with good and evil in the real world.

THE HERO, THE VILLAIN AND THE TRIUMPH OF GOODNESS

Every fairy tale has a protagonist or hero. This hero begins with a struggle or dilemma. He or she is often shown as weak and being abused by a higher authority or force; Cinderella and Snow White are examples. The hero has a problem to solve, task to perform or journey to embark on in order to overcome the evil force, personified in a villain. The hero's journey resembles and becomes our journey.

Bettelheim believes this to be one of the vital components of the fairy tale, helping children ponder and explore the meaning of life. He explains that the protagonist's travails teach the child some key lessons:

- Struggles and difficulties are part of life.
- Hardships are sometimes unexpected and unfair.
- We need to face our difficulties and roadblocks.

- We can master our difficulties and "emerge victorious."[9]

Amidst these struggles the hero must choose between good and evil. The battle of good and evil is a powerful theme as it is the same struggle we each face daily. In the fairy tale, good and evil are set up as polar opposites. A character is either all good or all evil. Snow White is good, and her stepmother, the witch, is evil. Dumbledore is good and Voldemort is evil. There is no middle ground. This use of polar opposites is effective with children because that is how they reason. Portraying the characters in accordance with children's black-and-white thinking allows them to easily distinguish between good and evil.[10]

The polar opposites presented in the Harry Potter books help children challenge the way they think of others and themselves. While Dumbledore may be all good and Voldemort all evil, some characters (like us) fall into the middle ground. For example, is Snape good or evil? He treats Harry unfairly and desperately wants to kill Sirius out of revenge, but on occasion he saves Harry's life, he is trusted by Dumbledore, and he is a member of the Order of the Phoenix. Children grow to realize that none of us humans are perfect (all good); we make mistakes and sometimes choose evil. But the polar opposites give us models. On our journeys we strive to be all good (Jesus) and avoid all evil (Satan). Our models help us to picture who we want—and don't want—to become.

The polar opposites also create a frame of reference by which to judge the hero's actions as she or he struggles to be good. Sometimes the hero is tempted by the villain or perhaps uses poor judgment and suffers a natural consequence that causes a setback. We can relate to the hero's mistakes and setbacks, and we are relieved when the hero gets back on track and learns from his or her lessons.

We see him or her striving to choose good, and we find comfort in the hero's lack of perfection because we aren't perfect either. We find assurance that we also can get back on track in our battle against evil.

Harry Potter is the hero of the Harry Potter books. His parents have been killed by the villain Lord Voldemort, and Harry has been raised by the mean, abusive Dursleys. The storyline closely resembles that of "Cinderella." Uncle Vernon and Aunt Petunia closely parallel Cinderella's evil stepmother. Harry is treated unfairly compared to Dudley, who is showered with praise, love and material gifts. Harry is ignored, mistreated and forced to wear rags that don't fit him. Dudley receives all the love, attention and material possessions, and he can do no wrong. Harry can do no right. Dudley picks on and abuses Harry, just as the stepsisters mistreat Cinderella. This begins in the first book and continues throughout the series.

As readers, we rejoice when the Dursleys get what is coming to them. One of my family's favorite examples occurs when Hagrid loses his temper with the Dursleys in *Harry Potter and the Sorcerer's Stone*. After Uncle Vernon insults Hogwarts and Dumbledore, Hagrid points his umbrella at Dudley.

> There was a flash of violet light, a sound like a firecracker, a sharp squeal, and the next second, Dudley was dancing on the spot with his hands clasped over his fat bottom, howling in pain. When he turned his back on them, Harry saw a curly pig's tail poking through a hole in his trousers.
>
> Uncle Vernon roared. Pulling Aunt Petunia and Dudley into the other room, he cast one last terrified look at Hagrid and slammed the door behind them.[12]

Harry is rescued from his predicament by Hagrid, who whisks him off to Hogwarts, where Harry becomes famous and finds friends. Hagrid, then, is like the fairy godmother who helps Cinderella go to the ball and gain the admiration of a prince. Cinderella finds love, happiness and a sense of belonging at the castle. In the same way, Harry finds happiness, love and belonging at Hogwarts. He dreads returning to the Dursleys' house, as Cinderella dreads returning to the home that has been taken over by her evil stepmother and stepsisters.

QUESTIONS TO BRIDGE THE GAP

- **Why do the Dursleys annoy us?**

- **Why are they so mean to Harry?**

- **Why does Dudley act like such a brat?**

- **Is it good to get everything you want? Why or why not?**

- **What would you do if you had to live with the Dursleys?**

- **When have you been treated unfairly? How did you feel? What did you do?**

However, the storyline of Harry Potter becomes considerably more complex as he encounters the evil forces of Lord Voldemort in the wizarding world and embarks on a journey of maturity in which he battles the three-headed dog, the troll and Voldemort. As a postmodern fairy tale, Harry Potter reflects the complexities that today's audience expects. For those who have ears to hear, it is a story with much to offer.

4

Discussing Fantasy
with Children

If we want our children to possess the traits of character we most
admire, we need to teach them what those traits are and why they
deserve both admiration and allegiance. Children must learn to
identify the forms and content of those traits. They must achieve
at least a minimal level of moral literacy that will enable them to
make sense of what they see in life and, we may hope, help them
live it well.

WILLIAM J. BENNETT, THE BOOK OF VIRTUES

One of the most enchanting aspects of the fairy tale for children is
the fact that it explores an imaginative, fantasy world. Children are allowed to enter a world of magical powers, charms and fascinating characters who are able to escape the boundaries of time and space. Their
imaginations are attracted to talking animals, mythological creatures
and recurrent symbols. One of the most recurrent symbols is the number three. You may have noticed that many stories feature three main
characters, three tests, three conflicts and so on. Scholars believe this
repetition of three reminds children of the basic family unit of mother,
father and child. They also find that it provides a soothing structural
refrain.[1] As Christians, we also see it as a symbol of the Trinity.

While it is natural to worry about children's embarking on imaginative adventures in a fantasy world, Bruno Bettelheim reassures us that that these magical journeys take children on deeper journeys into their unconscious self and allow them to return with an understanding of their conscious self.[2] While we often offer factual information to help children gain a understanding of the conscious self, this may not be enough. Bettelheim has found that children find understanding of themselves through

- daydreams

- pondering and fantasizing about stories

- relating fantasy stories to "unconscious pressures"

He believes fairy tales to "have unequaled value" because they allow children to add "new dimensions" to their imagination, structure their daydreams and find direction for life.[3]

Children (as well as adults) often repress and hide away fears and conflicts they don't want to face or do not understand. This causes stress and tension that are inevitably expressed in relationships and daily tasks. Repression is unhealthy and keeps us from living out our true potential. We need to work through our fears and struggles. Literature taps into our imagination and allows us to release our hidden fears and terrors—sometimes without our even realizing the release.

When the imagination is allowed to work out problems in the fantasy world of literature or daydreaming, the chances of the unconscious's "causing harm—to ourselves or others—is much reduced; some of its forces can then be made to serve positive forces."[4]

So the fantasy world of the fairy tale and Harry Potter sets before children the *necessary* task of working out their unconscious struggles and conflicts. It allows the unconscious to surface in a setting that reality does not provide. More important, the fairy tale encourages dialogue, thus fostering relationships that involve discussion of moral issues. "The child's enthusiasm for the story becomes contagious,"[5] as has been the case with the stories of Harry Potter. Adults are just as enthused about the Harry Potter books (if not more so) as children are.

Like the weavers of fairy tales, J. K. Rowling relies heavily on fantasy and magic to enchant her readers. At Hogwarts, Harry Potter enters a magical world where he uses a magical wand, flies on a broomstick and learns how to use witchcraft. It is important for us to remember that such fantasy is what makes the fairy tale so useful.

Children already think imaginatively. They daydream and engage in make-believe play to make sense out of their world. They do not operate on the same level of reasoning and principles of reality as adults do. As Bettelheim warns, it can be detrimental to personality development to repress children's use of fantasy worlds to make sense out of everyday life.

Children know that when they open up the Harry Potter books they are about to enter a different world with different rules. And when they close the book, they know that they have returned to reality. Opening the book in which a modern fairy tale is told serves the same purpose as the phrase "Once upon a time . . ." serves in the classic fairy tale.

We adults can ensure that our children understand the difference between reality and fantasy. The fantasy world is not something to be feared; rather, it is a useful tool for promoting moral growth and development.

In a world that uses fact to measure truth, the fantasy world of the fairy tale introduces children to deeper kinds of truth. Donald Baker labels this "the truth of experience, the intuitive feeling aroused when we contemplate some distant event or try to empathize with another human being."[6] This kind of truth can't be measured, seen or verified with tangible and concrete proofs. However, it is among the truths by which we make many of our moral decisions; it is the kind of truth that religious faith heavily relies on.

If we don't allow for our children to encounter this "truth of experience," how can we expect them to believe in a supernatural force that we call God? I am convinced that we should be more concerned about an education system that places all its emphasis on fact and seeks to strip imagination and faith from our children's learning than about a school system whose library includes fantasy literature.

LESSONS FROM A FANTASY WORLD

A good fantasy world contains valuable lessons about reality. The lessons are taught to us in an imaginative world that not only enchants us but also allows us to discover our fears, live through them with the characters and triumph over evil. Much of the controversy that surrounds the Harry Potter books focuses on their depiction of the use of magic to overcome evil and on Harry's being a wizard. Jack Zipes, a children's literature critic who does not like the Harry Potter series, even finds this ironic. In *Sticks and Stones* he calls Harry a "Christian Knight" and notes that the books are "clearly didactic and moralistic and preach against the evil use of magic."[7]

While magic, spells and special powers are used throughout Harry Potter and in some other fantasy literature, it is the character and moral virtues of the heroes and heroines that allow for good to win over evil—not the magic and fantasy. For example, we are repeatedly told that the *love* of Harry's mother protects him from Voldemort. That is why he continues to return to the real world and live with the Dursleys. In *Harry Potter and the Order of the Phoenix*, Dumbledore explains to Harry: "While you can still call home the place where your mother's blood dwells, there you cannot be touched or harmed by Voldemort. He shed her blood, but it lives on in you and her sister. Her blood became your refuge."[8]

Further, Dumbledore reveals that Harry possesses a force that Voldemort does not have or understand. He tells Harry, "That power saved you from possession by Voldemort because he could not bear to reside in a body so full of the force he detests. In the end, it mattered not that you could not close your mind. It was your heart that saved you."[9] Even in the fantastical world of Harry Potter, then, we find with our children that it is not magic that helps us defeat evil but love—a *real* gift given to us by God.

Love is real, but, like magic, it can't be apprehended by any of the five senses. By delving into the magical world of the fairy tale, we can learn to value, accept and feel a real faith in a God who can't be physically seen, touched, tasted, smelled or heard.

This should really not come as a surprise to us, as the fantastical world of the fairy tale actually is bent on introducing us to reality. This is especially true in the Harry Potter series, as we frequently travel between the Muggle world and the magical world. Especially through the character of Arthur Weasley, because of his fascination with the Muggle world, we get to look at our own world through an outsider's view. Not only does this

QUESTIONS TO BRIDGE THE GAP

- **The love of Harry's mother saved him, not magic. How do you know that you are loved?**

- **How do you share love with others?**

- **What does love feel like?**

- **Why is love more powerful than hate?**

- **We often hear that God is love. What does that mean to you?**

- **When has love helped or saved you?**

- **How did God's love save us?**

reconnect us with and ground us in reality, but it helps us sort out the differences between reality and fantasy.

For example, in *Harry Potter and the Chamber of Secrets,* Harry and the Weasley children use a car their father has collected from the Muggle world. In *Harry Potter and the Order of the Phoenix,* Arthur Weasley abandons magical medicine in an unsuccessful attempt to use stitches to close up his wound, and a telephone booth (reminiscent of Superman) doubles as an entry to the Ministry of Magic.

This traveling between two worlds is enjoyable and therapeutic. The journey gives us a better understanding of ourselves and our place in the world. In *Tending the Heart of Virtue: How Classic Stories Awaken a Child's Moral Imagination,* Orthodox theologian Vigen Guroian reminds us that such journeys allow children (and the rest of us) to take risks and practice making moral decisions without having to fully endure the painful consequences. We also get to experience joy and satisfaction in the positive outcomes of these moral choices. We get to celebrate our victories and mourn our losses. The fantasy world sharpens our moral imagination and prepares us for life. We return "transformed" as the characters met, battles fought and lessons learned stay with us. These "lasting images and metaphors," along with the guidance of parents and teachers, help form and shape children's morality and values.[10]

The Harry Potter books offer powerful examples of good and evil and show children how to love through the experiences of characters they have come to love and admire. In interaction with the Harry Potter books, children's (and adults') imaginations will begin to connect Harry's battles and adventures with their own battles in life. When Harry triumphs over Voldemort with love in *Harry Potter and the Order of the Phoenix,* we learn how love helps us gain victory over evil. "Fairy tales and modern fantasy stories project fantastic other worlds;

but they also pay close attention to real 'moral laws' of character and virtue."[11]

COMIC RELIEF

While some key theologians and educational theorists are confident that children can get home from Hogwarts on their own, others have concerns about a child's ability to discern reality and fantasy. Such concern is justified, as all children react differently and are reared in different environments. Thus it is good common sense for parents not only to know what children are reading but also enjoy it and discuss it with them. Great pleasure and bonding will occur through this sharing.

Reading literature with children and talking through it together empowers our children and helps them make sense of the world with our guidance. As we discuss the Harry Potter books with our children, we can make sure they understand that the magic in the stories is purely fictional and comical.

The magical elements in the stories are fun. They are part of the stories' enchantment. As Francis Bridger notes in *A Charmed Life: The Spirituality in the Potterworld*:

> The magic is preeminently a comic device. Its purpose is to elicit laughter, to make the viewer see the situation from a comedic perspective. . . . Magical happenings run through every chapter and a large part of their function is to play a joke on the reader. It is as if Joanne Rowling is saying to us: "O come on! Surely you don't take this stuff seriously?" If we fail to recognize the essential playfulness of Potterworld and magic's playful role in it, we shall have misread the series entirely. It can only be understood with a sense of humor.[12]

One example of magic as a comic device appears in *Harry Potter and the Prisoner of Azkaban.* We see magic here through the eyes of two of our most respected characters—Hermione and Professor McGonagall. We know Hermione to be intelligent, responsible and wise. Professor McGonagall is strict but also fair and compassionate. She is a sort of housemother of Gryffindor, and she cares about her house members.

After Divination class, in which Professor Trelawney predicts Harry's imminent death, her frightened students proceed stunned to Professor McGonagall's Transfiguration class. Puzzled, she asks them why her introductory transformation into a cat doesn't win her the usual applause. Hermione explains:

> "Please, Professor, we've just had our first Divination class, and we were reading the tea leaves, and—"

> "Ah, of course," said Professor McGonagall, suddenly frowning. "There is no need to say any more, Miss Granger. Tell me, which of you will be dying this year?"

> Everyone stared at her.

> "Me," said Harry, finally.

> "I see," said Professor McGonagall, fixing Harry with her beady eyes. "Then you should know, Potter, that Sibyll Trelawney has predicted the death of one student a year since she arrived at this school. None of them have died yet. Seeing death omens is her favorite way of greeting a new class. . . .

> "Divination is one of the most imprecise branches of magic. I shall not conceal from you that I have very little patience with it. . . .

> "You look in excellent health to me, Potter, so you will excuse

me if I don't let you off homework today. I assure you that if you die, you need not hand it in."[13]

Rowling describes Trelawney comically as resembling a "large, glittering insect," and her subsequent lessons are usually mocked by Harry, Ron and Hermione. When Ron asks Harry what he sees in Ron's tea leaves, Harry replies, "A load of soggy brown stuff."[14] Trelawney is not to be taken seriously, nor is her class. Even though she does make one correct prediction about Voldemort's return, even Dumbledore shows sincere surprise—displaying little confidence in Trelawney's abilities and class. Trelawney gives us a chance to laugh.

All good stories allow their readers to laugh once in a while. Besides giving us respite from the tension in the story, these moments teach us to find humor even during tough times—a valuable lesson.

QUESTIONS TO BRIDGE THE GAP

• **Professor Trelawney believes she can see into the future. Why don't Harry, Ron, Hermione and Professor McGonagall take her predictions seriously?**

• **Newspapers and magazines often include horoscopes. Sometimes it's amusing to read them. But why should we not take them seriously? How do they conflict with God's teachings?**

• **What do you think is the funniest magical scene in the book? Why?**

Clarifying Reality with Fantasy

The Harry Potter books provide us, of course, with opportunities to discuss the real occult and real witchcraft and what God teaches about such practices. A song by Chris Rice illustrates well our natural human tendency to want to solve problems with magic. Titled

"Magic Wand," it appears on his *Smell the Color 9* CD. I have used this song with my own children as well as in a third-grade classroom. Rice introduces us to a small child who watches a magician who often comes to town; the boy wishes he had a wand and magical powers to solve personal and world problems. As he grows and matures, the child realizes that the only way to "really change" is by making good everyday choices and obeying the Spirit of God whispering "within our soul." He grows to rely on the help of God and God's miracles.

Children love the catchy lyrics and make the connection easily. Rice's song acknowledges their wants and fantasies. It also reminds them that magic is not real. It doesn't solve problems and can never compare to the power of God—which is real!

Just so, through the course of the Harry Potter stories, we grow to realize that not even magic can solve Harry's problems. Magic rarely fixes things for him—and it surely didn't save his parents. Even the magical world of Hogwarts is haunted by death and loss.

QUESTIONS TO BRIDGE THE GAP

- **If you could be an animagus, what animal would you turn into? Why?**

- **When have you wished you had a magic wand?**

- **Harry and his friends have magic wands. Yet they still have problems. What are some of the problems that magic can't solve in the books?**

- **How could believing in God help Harry and his friends?**

- **How does God help us solve our problems?**

- **How do miracles differ from magic?**

The same is true for us. Magic cannot fix our problems. In fact, we often find that quick fixes only prolong our problems. We need to get to the root of our problems and find long-lasting, life-changing solutions. As Rice finds in his song, we need to make good choices and rely on the help of God.

FAIRY TALE STRUCTURE

A fun way to discuss fantasy literature with children and also foster critical thinking skills is to compare and contrast stories. This allows children to pick out differences, recognize similarities and practice making connections. It also reinforces the notion that these are *fictional* stories.

Fairy tales can be easily compared and contrasted with their common structure. Zipes gives us a paradigm in *Sticks and Stones.* He notes that the fairy tale has the following characteristics:

- An underdog, unaware of his or her talents, journeys to accomplish three goals.

- A forest or mysterious domain.

- A wise mentor, animals and friends who offer gifts and guidance.

- Adversaries, fantasy creatures, and obstacles to fight and conquer.

- Good wins over evil.[15]

Keeping these elements of the fairy tale in mind, you can draw on familiar stories as you read the Harry Potter books. For example, after pointing out the above elements in "Cinderella," you could ask your children to think about how a particular Harry Potter story is similar. Together you could then decide what elements recur in the formula or structure of the Harry Potter books. While Zipes finds the structure of Harry Potter books boring and predictable, children, as Bettelheim points out, find reassurance in fairy tales' repetitive structure. Children may also recognize that the Harry Potter books' plot lines follow the structure of the school year, and their own lives are structured around the school year as well!

In *The Pleasures of Children's Literature,* Perry Nodelman and Mavis Reimer encourage discussions that draw from a variety of stories. They find the fairy tale particularly useful, as it has common elements and a recognizable structure. "Shared plot," they say, "puts the variations, most of which imply different values, into sharp relief."[16]

The following list of stories can get you started comparing and contrasting the Harry Potter tales with other stories. Listing the elements of a fairy tale, create a chart with your children to help you visualize the similarities and differences (a sample chart appears on p. 50). Be sure to add the categories "fantasy" and "reality." Encourage the children to add to the list of stories and chart categories. You may want to put the chart on a large posterboard and hang it in the storytelling and reading area of your home or classroom. You could also do this in a reading journal.

"Cinderella"

"Little Red Riding Hood"

"Hansel and Gretel"

"Jack and the Beanstalk"

The Lion King

"Sleeping Beauty"

"Snow White"

A Bug's Life

101 Dalmatians

Robin Hood

"Beauty and the Beast"

Toy Story

Indiana Jones series

Star Wars series

Nancy Drew series

Hardy Boys series

The Chronicles of Narnia

The Lord of the Rings

A Wrinkle in Time series

The Three Musketeers

Common Characteristics	Cinderella	Harry Potter	Star Wars	Lord of the Rings
Heroine(s)				
Battle of Good vs. Evil/enemy				
Fantasy				
Reality				
Setting				
Theme/meaning				

TALKING ABOUT THE MOVIES

Another interesting topic of discussion is how the movies based on these stories differ from the original stories. Remember, a movie is based on a screenwriter's interpretation of the text, so it will vary from our own interpretations and sometimes even from the author's. Talk about how the director interpreted fantasy and reality. Did he or she come to the same conclusions as you?

For example, in the movie *Harry Potter and the Prisoner of Azkaban,* Hogwarts seems different from the way it looked and felt in the first two movies. What choices does the director make that give Hogwarts a different appearance? Do the characters look the way you imagined them? My children and I thought that in this movie there was much more attention to the outdoor landscaping. The scenery was beautiful, but it gave the movie a different feel. The lushness of nature, Hagrid's Hut and the rock archways reminded us of the Lord of the Rings film scenery.

While almost all of the characters looked just as we had pictured them, Sirius Black looked different from what we had imagined. We were also unhappy with the way Lupin looked when he turned into a werewolf. What characters did you picture differently?

For the sake of time, the director also made decisions about cutting material from the book. Do you think the cuts were made well? For example, the movie doesn't provide a clear explanation about how Hermione receives the hourglass. How might readers who have not read the books perceive the scene where Hermione and Harry go back in time? And would they understand Hermione's appearing out of nowhere in certain scenes? Such discussions are fun, and they build critical thinking skills in children.

5

Morals, Not Magic

It is most important that a child respect his parents, not for the purpose of satisfying their egos, but because the child's relationship with his parents provides the basis for his attitude toward all other people. . . . The conflict between generations occurs because of a breakdown in mutual respect, and it bears many painful consequences.

James Dobson, Dare to Discipline

Harry Potter and other stories give us fuel for moral discussion, but it is up to us to facilitate and guide that discussion. As you read Harry Potter with children, you may be surprised at the discussions that occur. Some children seem to make the connections between the stories and real life naturally. It is up to us to help them sort everything out.

While I was reading *Harry Potter and the Chamber of Secrets* with my children, my oldest daughter (five at the time) began a moral discussion about racial discrimination. It was stimulated by the scene where the Slytherin team invaded the Quidditch field so that Malfoy could gloat about his new position of seeker and the new Nimbus Two-thousand and One broomsticks his father had bought for the team.

Ron gaped, open-mouthed, at the seven superb broomsticks in front of him. "Good, aren't they?" said Malfoy smoothly. "But perhaps the Gryffindor team will be able to raise some gold and get new brooms too. You could raffle off those Cleansweep Fives; I expect a museum would bid for them."

The Slytherin team howled with laughter.

"At least no one on the Gryffindor team had to *buy* their way in," said Hermione sharply. "*They* got in on pure talent."

The smug look on Malfoy's face flickered.

"No one asked your opinion, you filthy little Mudblood," he spat.

Harry knew at once that Malfoy had said something really bad because there was an instant uproar at his words.[1]

Ron heroically stands up for Hermione and shoots his wand at Malfoy. Unfortunately, however, the spell backfires, and Ron starts spitting up slugs. Harry and Hermione take Ron to Hagrid's, where they have the following discussion about "Mudbloods."

"So tell me," said Hagrid, jerking his head at Ron. "Who was he tryin' ter curse?"

"Malfoy called Hermione something—it must've been really bad, because everyone went wild."

"It *was* bad," said Ron hoarsely, emerging over the tabletop looking pale and sweaty. "Malfoy called her 'Mudblood,' Hagrid—"

Ron dived out of sight again as a fresh wave of slugs made their appearance. Hagrid looked outraged.

"He didn't," he growled at Hermione.

"He did," she said. "But I don't know what it means. I could tell it was really rude, of course—"

"It's about the most insulting thing he could think of," gasped Ron, coming back up. "Mudblood's a really foul name for someone who is Muggle-born—you know, non-magic parents. There are some wizards—like Malfoy's family—who think they're better than everyone else because they're what people call pure-blood." He gave a small burp, and a single slug fell into his outstretched hand. He threw it into the basin and continued, "I mean, the rest of us know it doesn't make any difference at all. Look at Neville Longbottom—he's pureblood and he can hardly stand a cauldron the right way up."

"An' they haven't invented a spell our Hermione can' do," said Hagrid proudly, making Hermione go a brilliant shade of magenta.[2]

After hearing this passage, my daughter interrupted and asked, "Mom, why can't people get along? Why do they care if people are different?"

Stunned by the connection she had made at the age of five, I looked and her and paused. Then I responded. "That is a good question, Brianna." We went back to the beginning of the scene, and I broke it down with the following questions.

- Why do you think Malfoy called Hermione that name?
  He was jealous and afraid.

- Why would he be jealous of Hermione?
  She is smart.

- Why would he be afraid of Hermione?
  Hermione said Malfoy had his father buy the brooms so he could be seeker. The kids may think he isn't a good seeker. He is afraid Hermione is smarter than he is.

- Why do you think "purebloods" came up with the term *Mudblood*?

> *To make wizards that are different from purebloods feel bad.*

- Why would they want them to feel bad?

  They are afraid of them.

At this point, my daughter brought up what had really been bothering her. Some children in her daycare were being mean to a friend of a different ethnicity. Brianna was upset that the other children were being unkind to her friend. She didn't see any negative difference in her friend, nor did we. So we talked about the situation in relation to the discussion we had just had about Hermione and Malfoy.

- How are the daycare kids acting like Malfoy?

  They are being mean to my friend. They are calling her names and won't let her play with us.

- Why do you think they treat her this way?

  Because she is different, and they want her to feel bad.

Once we reached this point, I helped her understand the connection further. I said: "Sometimes people fear what is different from them. This causes a lot of pain and suffering in our world. Just as Malfoy and the pureblood wizards fear Hermione because she is different, some people in our world fear people of different races and mixed races. Oftentimes their fear leads to hate. Like Ron, Harry and Hagrid, we know this is wrong. We need to continue to reach out to those who are mistreated, respect others and speak out when people are treated unfairly."

We then broke into a discussion about how to act in situations where people are treated unfairly. We discussed how Ron responded. While his intentions were good, he reacted out of anger and lost his temper. This had negative consequences for him. My children and I decided that his walking away with Hermione might have spoken much louder than violence or words. Brianna decided that when the daycare kids treated her friend badly in the future, she would not argue with them but would just walk away with her friend and play something else.

Encountering this part of the story with my children provided an opportunity for us to engage in a moral discussion about discrimination. It also let me know what was going on at daycare and how Brianna felt about it. Together we worked through her feelings and arrived at a solution for handling the problem. I might not have had this opportunity had I not read Harry Potter with her and her siblings that night.

THEORIES OF MORAL DEVELOPMENT

Reading Harry Potter with children provides many such openings to build the type of relationship that will foster moral development. As Christian parents, we need to understand how children progress through the stages of moral development and how literature and Christian teachings work to foster that moral development.

Both Jean Piaget and Lawrence Kohlberg found that moral development occurs in stages. While their theories of the stages are somewhat different, they agree that moral development begins with an understanding of good and bad. Young children realize that there are both bad and good consequences to their actions, and they begin to take these consequences into account when they choose to act.

Piaget and Kohlberg agree that in the first level of moral development, parents are seen as enforcers of discipline. Parents are authoritarian figures who judge behavior as good or bad and use punishments and rewards to help the child decipher what behavior is good and bad. Punishment indicates bad behavior, and reward indicates good and desirable behavior. For example, when a child hears "Cheating is bad," the child reasons, *If I cheat, I'll be punished.* In this stage, adults are seen as bigger, stronger and different. Not surprisingly, children in this stage often feel like outsiders in society.[3]

Piaget and Kohlberg also agree that children must pass through stages of moral development in order to arrive at a higher stage of moral reasoning, which these theorists both call *autonomous morality.*[4] Autonomous morality is independent of external pressures and is marked by acts of respect and consideration for others. At this level of morality, we are not governed by written laws or rules; we respond with empathy to the needs of others. Immanuel Kant's categorical imperative and Christianity's Golden Rule are examples of autonomous reasoning; both teach that one should not do to others what one would not want done to oneself. Our goal is to help children achieve autonomous morality—to grow up into critical thinkers who can make moral choices.[5]

Piaget found that parents often hinder their children from achieving autonomous morality by reinforcing rules that focus only on external consequences.[6] If parents don't encourage critical thinking that fosters "participation in formulating morality,"[7] he warns, children may never achieve autonomous morality or may turn to their peers for morality formation.

When a parent-child relationship remains at the level of choices reinforced by external consequences, the child may grow up to be self-absorbed. In order to understand how others feel and realize their role in society, children must be able to role-play. They need to think about how others feel and see the purposes behind rules and customs.[8]

As discussed earlier, the stories of Harry Potter allow our children to do exactly what Kohlberg proposes: role-play and understand how others feel. By reading and discussing Harry Potter with children, we help them understand what it means to be a part of society. From feeling themselves to be outsiders, they begin to consider themselves an essential part of society—just as Harry Potter moves from being an outcast and orphan to become a hero and friend.

Like our children, Harry, Ron and Hermione often question and break rules. While reading the books, our children find that even at Hogwarts breaking rules results in negative consequences. Often, however, it is natural rather than imposed consequences that reveal the reason for the rules and show that authority figures often have our best interests in mind. Here are just a few examples:

QUESTIONS TO BRIDGE THE GAP

- **What is one rule at home you really dislike? Why?**

- **What is the reason for that rule?**

- **When have you broken that rule? What happened?**

- **What would happen if you didn't have that rule?**

- **How do you know the difference between a good rule and a bad rule?**

- **What can you do if there is a bad rule at home? at school? in the city? the state? the country? the world?**

- **What are some bad rules from the past that have been changed? Who helped change those rules? What did they do to get them changed?**

- Ron and Harry fly the Weasleys' car to Hogwarts without permission. They are beaten up by the whomping willow and reprimanded by Professor McGonagall; Ron's father gets in trouble with the Ministry of Magic, and Ron receives a howler. They realize that they made a poor choice.

- Hermione makes an advanced "polyjuice" potion so she, Harry and Ron can disguise themselves and get some information from Malfoy. Because a cat hair is used in the potion, however, Hermione is transformed into a cat. She learns that perhaps she wasn't ready to be making advanced potions and shouldn't be transforming herself into someone else.

- Ginny doesn't tell anyone about Tom Riddle's journal and her communication with him. After she almost loses her life, she learns not to keep secrets that endanger herself and others.

- Acting out of fear, Harry attempts to communicate with Sirius Black with Floo powder but gets caught by Professor Umbridge. He realizes that his actions have jeopardized the plans of the Order of the Phoenix and put Sirius at risk. Harry later blames himself for Sirius's death.

Psychologist Martin Hoffman suggests four experiences for fostering autonomous morality in children: (1) Expose children to challenging experiences and allow them to face the consequences of their actions. (2) Let children role-play, and provide opportunities for them to care for others. (3) Help children empathize with others. (4) Provide children with positive role models who demonstrate autonomous morality.[9] These experiences of moral development accord well with the theories of Kohlberg and Piaget. Following are some ideas for using them as you share Harry Potter with your children.

DEALING WITH CONSEQUENCES

Expose children to the real-life issues and struggles that arise in the Harry Potter stories, and encourage them to imagine themselves in those situations and role-play moral solutions and responses. Together you can assess the choices that are being made and relate them to similar situations in your own lives. When discussing the moral issues, first guide children to an understanding of the issue, then explore possibilities for appropriate resolution. Help your children decide on appropriate actions to take when faced with a similar situation.[10]

For example, when Harry is punished unjustly by Professor Snape in chapter eight of *Harry Potter and the Sorcerer's Stone,* you might use questions like these to help children arrive at a suitable moral course of action:

- How does Professor Snape treat Harry fairly or unfairly?

- What do you think Harry should do? Why?

- When have you been treated unfairly by a teacher? What did you do to resolve the conflict? How successful were you?

- What can a student do when he or she is being treated unfairly by a teacher?

Note that these questions aim first at interpreting the moral conflict and then move toward a practical resolution that also applies to everyday life. As you reflect on these questions with children, participate actively in the discussion by sharing your own struggles, experiences, stories and resolutions. For example, you could recount a time when you were treated unfairly by a teacher and explain what you did to resolve the conflict. Discuss your choices, even if they weren't the right choices at the time. Children will find comfort and reassurance in the fact that you struggled with moral choices just as they are struggling. And in fact, it is important to let them know that you are still struggling.

Avoid taking on the authoritarian voice of a teacher as you talk about moral choices. Remember, you are striving to help your children move beyond moral reasoning that relies on the approval and rewards of adults. Listen to your children's responses and guide them with questions that challenge their reasoning skills. Help them arrive at a moral response on their own.

If you are reading and talking with children of various ages, keep in mind that they may be at different levels of moral development and may have different responses. Some younger children may respond to Harry's conflict with Professor Snape by asserting that all questioning of a teacher is "bad" because it could bring punishment. Some of the older children will understand that adults make mistakes too and that as members of a community and society we need to respect each other. Thus children are entitled to fair and equal treatment, just as adults are. Further, children have the responsibility and right to respectfully question any actions of adults that seem unfair or abusive.

If you are discussing these issues with a variety of age groups, the variety of responses will encourage all the children to think about and challenge their own reasoning—and this can help them develop a higher level of moral reasoning.

Remember, it is your interaction and facilitation in the discussion that will guide them in their moral development. If they catch you off guard, as children sometimes do, it is always OK to say, "That's a good question. Let me think about that for a while." This gives you time to think about and research the best way of handling the question. It also shows your children that adults don't always have all the answers and that some questions and situations require extra time and thought.

OPPORTUNITIES FOR ROLE-PLAY

A wide variety of activities can help your children apply the story of Harry Potter, chapter by chapter, to everyday life: helping others, role-playing the characters, researching real-life issues, creative art projects, games and so on. This will give you and your children the chance to put your moral development into practice. This is an important component of sharing the story because moral development not only includes thought and emotion; it also includes behavior.

Use the moral lessons of Harry Potter as launching pads for activities of service. These will give children practice putting moral lessons into action. Here are a few possibilities for helping children role-play, show care and concern for others and connect the stories with real life.

- Hermione knits socks to help free the house elves. Encourage children to brainstorm ways they can help combat unfair treatment of others. Perhaps you could arrange to serve in a soup kitchen.

- Harry Potter is set in England. Research customs and traditions of England. Prepare and enjoy an afternoon tea together.

- Children love to compare the various houses of Hogwarts and talk about where they would fit in. Come up with a name for your household or classroom. Make a poster listing house rules that foster respect.

- Hagrid is skilled at caring for animals. Adopt a pet, or volunteer to help out at an animal shelter.

Your children will learn that even at a very young age, they too can make a difference. They also can share God's word with others. All of this from Harry Potter!

Sheltering children from society and reinforcing behavior exclusively with external punishments only retard moral development. Role-playing, imagination, critical thinking and strong parent-child relationships are crucial if children are to grow into thoughtful, mature moral adults. As we share Harry Potter books and other literature with them, we can unlock doors that will open up to a lifelong journey of moral growth.

IN ANOTHER'S SHOES

Together, talk about the fantastical aspects of each chapter. Enjoy the fantasy world of Harry Potter. Stimulate moral development by allowing children to "imagine themselves in the place of others." Yet at the same time, help children bridge the gap between fantasy and reality. Discuss how Hogwarts differs from home. For example, "Harry tries to solve his problems with magic. Why is magic not a real solution for our problems? What steps can we take to solve problems?"

Many critics of Harry Potter fear his imaginative world. But in actuality, it is the imaginative world of Harry Potter as a realm for the classic battle of good and evil that makes it such fertile planting ground for moral development. Harry Potter attracts our minds to the fantasy world and draws us into his struggles with friendship, peer pressure, child abuse, greed and evil. We experience his pain when battling the Dursleys, Snape and Malfoy, and we triumph when he chooses good over evil and defeats Lord Voldemort.

Children's imaginations are well harnessed and channeled with stories that offer a victorious hero who chooses good over evil. They can fall in love with this moral hero and decide that they also want to choose good over evil. When Christian parents help them see the Christian parallels present in the Harry Potter stories, children will be encouraged to take up the battle against the evils of Satan in their lives.

ROLE MODELS OF AUTONOMOUS MORALITY

As you discuss the Harry Potter books in relation to Scripture, your children will be challenged to examine their lives in light of the teachings of Christ. In your discussions, don't be afraid to ask, "What would Jesus do?" Then when they are faced with a similar situation in real life, they can seek to do what Jesus would do.

For example, Professor Snape introduces himself in Potions class to his students by saying, "I can teach you how to bottle fame, brew glory, even stopper death."[11] You may want to pause and ask, "What do Snape's teachings value? What did Jesus' teachings value? What do you value? What do Christians value?"

Questions such as these help us to examine cultural messages and filter life through a Christian lens, so that we learn not only to think like Christ but also how to love and forgive like Christ.

6

THE REAL ISSUES IN HARRY POTTER

There's a fundamental realism to him, a vulnerability, without
which he would never have appealed to both children and adults in
the way he has. At the end of the day, Harry is neither devil nor
saint—he's essentially "the boy who lived."

FRANCIS BRIDGER, *A CHARMED LIFE:*
THE SPIRITUALITY OF THE POTTERWORLD

One of the reasons we love Harry so much is because he is a lot like us. He struggles through the difficulties of every day just as we do. Children especially find that they have a lot in common with Harry.

As you discuss some of the real-life issues Harry faces, you have an opportunity to help children sort out reality from fantasy. Usually these issues will present themselves as you read the books. The ways they apply to each adult and child will be different, as we each carry our own life experiences and struggles. Here are just a few of the issues that you may want to discuss as you read the texts:

- child abuse: the Dursleys' treatment of Harry

- family structure and relationships: the Dursleys versus the Weasleys versus the Malfoys

- bullying: Crabbe, Goyle, Malfoy, Dudley

- sibling rivalry: the Weasley children, Harry and Dudley
- materialism and economic status: the Weasleys and Malfoys
- teacher-student relations: Professor Snape's treatment of Harry; Professor's Umbridge's treatment of students and discipline strategies
- good versus evil: the fight against Lord Voldemort and the Death Eaters
- love: friendships formed, family relations, Harry and Sirius, Hagrid, the love that protects Harry
- fear: how the children respond to the tasks and battles fought; fear of death, fear of the forest, Ron's fear of losing, fear of Hagrid's brother, fear of saying Voldemort's name, fear of bullies, fear of gangs
- rules: rules at home, rules at school, society rules, moral and Christian rules
- discipline: appropriate discipline versus abusive discipline; Dumbledore versus Umbridge; McGonagall versus Snape; abuse of power
- gangs: Dudley and his friends; Malfoy and his thugs
- prejudice/racism: Mudbloods, Death Eaters, house elves
- death penalty: the dementors, Azkaban, kiss of death, Sirius Black, Buckbeak
- life after death: ghosts at Hogwarts, Nearly Headless Nick, Harry's parents, Sirius Black, Cedric
- risk taking: rule breaking, fighting Voldemort, going into the forest

- magic/occult: the stories versus society versus Scripture

- loss of parents/loved ones: Harry's parents, Neville's parents, Sirius Black, Cedric

- running away from home and life problems: Sirius; Harry's temptation to run from home and Hogwarts

- friendship: the various friendships formed; good friends versus bad friends

- family values: Weasleys, Blacks, Potters, Nevilles, Malfoys, Grangers

- religion and faith: battle of good versus evil; all issues in relation to Scripture teachings

As you engage in discussions with children, keep in mind that they will be much more likely to respond if you treat their opinions and responses with respect. The atmosphere should be open and casual. Don't give the impression that there is a right answer or that they are being quizzed. You should begin the discussion and offer your feelings and opinions openly. Tell stories from your own life that relate to the story. Don't be afraid to disagree.

At the same time, as the facilitator, you need to keep a good balance. While it is important to respect and be open to children's opinions and responses, some issues require a voice of authority and strong guidance. Don't fall into the trap of trying to be their best friend. You are a guardian and respected adult. As professors of children's literature Perry Nodelman and Mavis Reimer remind us, "Respecting the response of others doesn't necessarily mean not admitting to disagreements with them."[1] We do well to stay focused on our main responsibility—guiding, directing and raising Christian children with a developed moral sensibility.

FOR THE LOVE OF READING

Nodelman and Reimer provide some helpful pointers to keep in mind when reading with our children. While all children are different, use these findings to help guide your discussions. They note that most readers

- are not motivated by how quickly or how much they can read. They are in love with the story.

- don't read everything with the same focus. While they may pay great attention to detail one day, they may glance through sections the next day.

- enjoy questioning the ideas and messages presented.

- enjoy continuing interaction and dialogue with others who are also reading the text.[2]

When reading with my children, I sometimes stop in the middle of the story with a question. For example, when we first encountered Snape's unfair treatment of Harry in Potions class, I stopped and said, "Wow. That would be tough to deal with! How would you react if a teacher treated you unfairly?"

After listening to the children's responses, I talked about how I felt when I was treated unfairly at school. One day in third grade, as I stood in the recess line, the teacher saw that I had mud on my shoes and decided I should write a one-hundred-word report on mud. Others also had mud on their shoes because it was a rainy day, but only I was singled out to receive a frowning worm and write an essay. I felt very angry that I had been treated unfairly. In fact, I frequently felt picked on by that teacher. This is normal and happens to every child at some point during school. We need to realize that others don't define who we are. I wrote the essay and moved on. I was happy to have a new teacher in fourth grade.

My children and I continued talking about the differences between necessary and fair rules and unfair and abusive treatment of children by school authorities. I gave them suggestions for dealing with problems at school.

It is hard for children to sort out fair and unfair treatment, so discussions like this one provide much-needed direction and encourage them to discuss school struggles with you. You are talking about the issue in the text of a story they enjoy; the emphasis is not on them but on Harry. This makes the discussion both easier and more enjoyable. You will find that children love to tell their own stories and articulate their ideas. My children have had many applicable and interesting stories to tell. And our Harry Potter discussions have encouraged them to talk to me throughout the day about what they're going through—not just during storytime.

Your children may stop you as you read to comment on something or ask a question. Fantasy stories stimulate our imaginations and help us to dream. Encourage their questions and praise their observations! You're finding out what is on their minds and how they are responding to the story, and such discussions promote critical thinking skills and bring you closer to each other.

It can be a good idea to read ahead so that you can anticipate questions and responses. Never underestimate your children. Always be prepared!

The following chapters survey many of the themes present in the Harry Potter books. These themes provide opportunities for discussing real issues and situations with children and connecting the stories with their Christian faith. During these discussions, children may open up and reveal traumas, fears, anger and other strong feelings.

Questions have been provided to get you talking. Use them as a guide, but don't hesitate to deviate from them or to add your own. You may need to adjust them to the maturity level and ages of your children. Rowling has suggested that her books' best readers are children the same age as Harry. I have read some of them to my children at younger ages because they were interested and I knew they could handle it. Other young children may not be ready. You will need to make that decision.

PART TWO

TALKING ABOUT HARRY POTTER
WITH YOUR CHILDREN

7

Dealing with Traumatic Experiences

*Numbing the pain for a while will make
it worse when you finally feel it.*

PROFESSOR DUMBLEDORE, *HARRY POTTER
AND THE GOBLET OF FIRE*

Sometimes moral growth comes in the midst of tragedy. As they grow and develop, children must deal with the same traumas of daily living that we adults face. Life is not always fair. In fact, sometimes it is harsh and cruel. Children need help making sense of these situations. They need outlets for their stress, fear and anxiety. They need to heal.

Harry Potter gives us opportunities to help our children open up and talk about the difficult times that they have faced and still must face. As an orphan living in an abusive home, Harry struggles with many different emotions. He often wants to talk, but in the Muggle world there is no one to listen to him. One morning Harry wakes up from a bad dream with his scar hurting. He is afraid, confused and lonely.

Harry went restlessly back to the bed and sat down on it, running a finger over his scar again. It wasn't the pain that bothered him;

Harry was no stranger to pain and injury. He had lost all the bones from his right arm once and had them painfully regrown in a night. The same arm had been pierced by a venemous foot-long fang not long afterward. Only last year Harry had fallen fifty feet from an airborne broomstick. He was used to bizarre accidents and injuries; they were unavoidable if you attended Hogwarts School of Witchcraft and Wizardry and had a knack for attracting a lot of trouble. . . .

Harry shook himself mentally; he was being stupid. There was no one in the house with him except Uncle Vernon, Aunt Petunia, and Dudley, and they were plainly still asleep. . . . Harry had never been able to confide in them or tell them anything about his life in the wizarding world.[1]

Many children feel much the same. They feel trapped in an unfair and cruel world with no one to turn to. Harry gives children hope and courage. If Harry can deal with such horrendous circumstances and succeed, so can they. And they have us to help them through it.

The traumatic experiences children face vary in nature and degree, of course. Sometimes our children face multiple stresses. Harry has dealt with extraordinary circumstances, such as "losing all the bones in his right arm" and "having them painfully regrown in one night" and then having the same arm "pierced by a venomous foot-long fang." He has also fallen fifty feet from a broomstick. While these injuries are fantastical, children who have experienced a broken arm or loss of a limb identify with them. A child who has been bitten by a snake or fallen from a tree or window may also be able to relate. And *all* children know what it's like to wake up from a nightmare and feel as if it was real. Some children feel alone and isolated, without parents or anyone they feel they can confide in.

Sadly, children encounter family deaths, sexual abuse, physical abuse, war, large-scale tragedies like the attack on the Twin Towers, bullying, divorce, fires, floods, tornadoes, hurricanes, crime. We know that all of these traumatic events take place, but we seldom associate them with childhood. We think of childhood as the age of innocence and play; we don't want to think of children as experiencing the same cruelties we face as adults. Yet our children do share our traumas and distress. Other less serious but still painful challenges include starting a new school, moving to a new city, a friend's moving away or the death of a pet. Such situations cause strong emotions in children. As much as we want to shelter them from pain and suffering, we can't.

QUESTIONS TO BRIDGE THE GAP

- **How do you feel when you wake up from a bad dream? Why?**

- **What was one of your worst dreams?**

- **What did you do to feel better?**

- **Who is someone you can talk to when you are really afraid?**

- **How does that person make you feel safe?**

But we can help them heal. They need to open up and talk about how they feel with a trusted adult. Delving into books like the Harry Potter series with children is a unique way to help them begin to heal from their hurt. And in the process, we may find ourselves healing as well.

Through the process of healing you will find that children's reactions to stress vary in degree and form depending on many factors, including the stress, the child's personality, family support and genetic predisposition. Reactions often include depression, anxiety and physical illness. In some cases, children may even develop posttraumatic stress disorder (PTSD); they may engage in play and behavior reenacting the event or suffer frightening nightmares, headaches, stomachaches and other psychosomatic physical pain. They may undergo anxiety and extreme distress when they encounter triggers that remind them of the trauma.[2] They need our help to find a way to cope with what life has tossed at them.

To adequately help children experiencing symptoms such as these, you may need to get support and advice from a clinical psychologist, psychiatrist, pediatrician or school counselor. But you may be able to help the traumatized child take the first step to opening up and healing.

Another important lesson is conveyed as you share literature with your children: they learn that they are loved. When we spend time sharing stories with children, listening to their needs and thoughts, and having fun with them, they feel loved. This also shows them how to love—to listen to others and care about their needs. How we treat our children often determines how they will treat others. Michael Schulman and Eva Mekler tell us in their book *Bringing Up a Moral Child,* "The evidence is quite clear on this. . . . Parents who spent time playing, conversing, joking with, and reading with their children had children who were friendly, generous and affectionate."[3]

We need to find ways to build resilience in our children, so that they can cope more effectively when they face hardships and struggle with fear. The following chapters will explore ways to build inner strength and flexibility through Harry Potter discussions.

8

FACING FEARS

Harry thought . . . What scared him most in the world?

HARRY POTTER AND THE PRISONER OF AZKABAN

Reading and discussing literature such as the Harry Potter books with children helps them face their fears and become more resilient. The stories allow them to identify with characters who are coping with situations of stress and anxiety. Additionally, reading and discussing the story with children will build autonomy, critical thinking skills and self-esteem. They can role-play various coping strategies that they can use when they face struggles and conflicts.

Many of the stresses children deal with are portrayed within the Harry Potter stories. For example, Harry Potter copes with the violent death of his parents. Children who have lost parents or witnessed a violent murder will be able to relate with Harry's loss and fears. In fact Harry demonstrates many of the symptoms of PTSD. He has frequent nightmares, unexplained physical pain (his scar repeatedly hurts), anger and flashbacks. In reading the books and discussing his plight, children who are experiencing PTSD not only will be able to relate to Harry but will find opportunities to discuss their symptoms with a trusted adult.

Even children who have not experienced such a traumatic event will be able to work out their fears and anxieties about facing a similar tragedy. Children often fear losing their parents. Discussing Harry's struggles allow these hidden fears to be uncovered, released and resolved.

Due to the richness and complexity of the books, other stresses also surface for discussion. Ron Weasley struggles with his family's lack of money. Hermione deals with prejudice and discrimination. Harry is treated unfairly and abused by teachers.

In *Harry Potter and the Prisoner of Azkaban,* Professor Lupin tells his students that boggarts come out of dark closets and other hiding places to take on people's worst fears. In order to battle the boggart, the wizard must think of his or her worst fear in a humorous manner. For example, Neville Longbottom's worst fear is Professor Snape, so he pictures Snape dressed as his grandmother.

QUESTIONS TO BRIDGE THE GAP

• **What is your worst fear?**

• **What shape would a boggart take as it approached you?**

• **How could you imagine the thing you fear in a funny way?**

My son hates shots, so he said that a boggart would take the form of a needle. He pictured the needle as a giant squeaky toy chasing the nurse around the room.

This exercise can also be moved up to a spiritual level. Often we fear things when we don't have trust in God. Ask children, "How could you turn your fear over to God?" After they respond, allow them a few minutes to silently turn their fears over to God.

9

Battling Bullies

Harry and Ron made furious moves toward Malfoy,
but Hermione got there first—SMACK!

Harry Potter and the Prisoner of Azkaban

One conflict central to all of the Harry Potter books is bullying. This conflict is also central in our children's lives. We need to build relationships of trust with our children, so that we will know when they are dealing with a bully. Likewise, we need to know if our children are bullying others. It's important to teach them to respect others and to give them effective strategies for dealing with bullies.

When you talk about bullying as you read the Harry Potter stories, your children will not feel that the focus of the conversation is on them. This means they will be more open about their struggles. They may connect the stories readily to their own situation and reveal the bullies they are dealing with.

If not, you may need to probe a little once the conversation begins with questions like "What would you do if you had to deal with someone like Draco Malfoy?" or "When have you acted like Draco Malfoy?" It is important that you listen to what they share and respond without judgment. You could tell about a time that you dealt with a bully and explain how you resolved the issue. You could also suggest proactive strategies for dealing with the issue.

Barbara Coloroso, internationally recognized speaker on parenting, teaching, positive school climate, nonviolent conflict resolution and grieving, affirms the significance of discussing conflicts with children. She suggests that children practice and discuss problem-solving skills together: "Kids who have solved problems successfully together are more likely to come to each other's aid when either is being bullied."[1]

When your reading brings you to one of Harry, Hermione and Ron's difficult conflicts with Draco Malfoy and his gang (and there are many!), use problem-solving steps to discuss a peaceful resolution to the conflict. These are the problem-solving steps offered by Coloroso:

1. Identify and define the problem.
2. List viable options for solving the problem.
3. Evaluate the options; explore the pros and cons of each one.
4. Choose one option.
5. Make a plan and carry it out.
6. Evaluate the problem and your solution: What brought it about? Could a similar problem be prevented in the future? How was the problem solved?[2]

In *Harry Potter and the Order of the Phoenix,* Malfoy and his fellow Slytherins harass and bully Harry and the Weasleys after Harry has captured the Golden Snitch and Gryffindor has won a Quidditch match.

> Harry heard a snort from behind him and turned around, still holding the Snitch tightly in his hand: Draco Malfoy had landed close by; white-faced with fury, he was still managing to sneer.
>
> "Saved Weasley's neck, haven't you?" he said to Harry. "I've never seen a worse Keeper . . . but then he was *born in a bin.* . . .

Did you like my lyrics, Potter?"

Harry did not answer; he turned away to meet the rest of the team who were now landing one by one, yelling and punching the air in triumph.[3]

Here is how you and your children might figure out a resolution to this conflict using Coloroso's problem-solving steps.

Problem: The Slytherin team is jealous that Gryffindor won the match. Slytherin team members have decided to take their anger out on Harry and Ron by insulting them.

Options

Ignore the insults. Pro: You will not be punished for fighting. Con: Malfoy and the others may continue to harass and yell insults. Hostility will continue in the future.

Ignore the insults and leave the playing field. Pro: You will not be punished and will not hear the insults anymore. The Slytherin team will be frustrated at the fact that you did not respond to their meanness. Con: None.

Yell insults back. Pro: You may feel satisfaction at bothering them. Con: You will enrage them further and provoke a fight. You risk being injured in the fight, and you may be punished by school administrators.

Fight the Slytherin team. Pro: None. Con: You may be injured. They may be injured. You will be punished. There will be continued hostility in the future.

Choose option: *Ignore the insults and leave the playing field.*

Make a plan: As a team, walk away from the field and ignore the insults.

Evaluate: The Gryffindor team shows maturity by ignoring the insults and avoiding further conflict.

Unfortunately, this is not the solution the Gryffindor players choose. While they do ignore the insults in the beginning, they remain on the field and allow themselves to become enraged to the point of battle. After Harry and George fight Malfoy, Malfoy and George are injured; Harry and George are punished. Malfoy and the Slytherin team get away without any punishment.

> "What do you think you're doing?" screamed Madam Hooch.
> . . . Malfoy was curled up on the ground, whimpering and moaning, his nose bloody; George was sporting a swollen lip; Fred was still being forcibly restrained by the three Chasers, and Crabbe was cackling in the background.
>
> "I've never seen behavior like it—back up to the castle, both of you, and straight to your Head of House's office! Go! *Now!*[4]

Obviously, Harry and George do not choose the best option. Rather than ignoring the insults and walking away, they allow themselves to be provoked into a fight. In the end, they are punished—which is exactly what the Slytherins wanted.

Talking through conflicts such as this and teaching problem-solving steps gives children experience and foresight for peacefully resolving conflicts. Not only does this build independence and self-esteem, but it shows them that problems are best solved in cooperation. They also learn that there may be several ways to effectively solve a problem.

10

DELVING INTO DIVERSITY

We are only as strong as we are united, as weak as we are divided.

PROFESSOR DUMBLEDORE, *HARRY POTTER*
AND THE GOBLET OF FIRE

P arents' attitudes are contagious. As you read through the Harry
Potter books, you can encourage children to be aware of and learn
about others' cultures. Often you will find it natural to break into discussions about cultural diversity and celebrate differences. With
older children, you will also find opportunities to talk about histori-
cal mistakes and tragedies that occurred because of intolerance and
ignorance. *Harry Potter and the Goblet of Fire* is rich in opportunities
for both. Allow the sharing of your children to guide the depth of
these discussions.

In *Harry Potter and the Goblet of Fire,* Harry and his friends learn
about the cultures and differences of others through the Quidditch
World Cup and the visits of the Beauxbatons and Durmstrang. While
reading this book, my children eagerly offered what they had learned
about their friends who came from various non-Anglo cultures. As
the Beaubatons and Durmstrang children spoke in different accents
and languages, my children interrupted to share the various words
they knew in other languages.

Sometimes we may be frightened of others' differences or hesitant to try a food or custom of a different culture. In the following scene, Rowling humorously uses Ron to show a common reaction to a food of another country. Use the scene and the questions that follow to explore your knowledge of and reactions to others' cultures.

There was a greater variety of dishes in front of them than Harry had ever seen, including several that were definitely foreign.

QUESTIONS TO BRIDGE THE GAP

- **How does Ron react to the foreign foods? Why?**

- **How does Hermione react?**

- **Who seems more open to other cultures' foods and customs? How can you tell? How might education and knowledge have something to do with this?**

- **When have you tried a food from another country? How did you feel about it?**

- **What are some of your favorite foreign foods?**

- **Why is it important to be open to others' foods and customs?**

"What's *that*?" said Ron, pointing at a large dish of some sort of shellfish stew that stood beside a large steak-and-kidney pudding.

"Bouillabaisse," said Hermione.

"Bless you," said Ron.

"It's *French*," said Hermione. "I had it on holiday summer before last. It's very nice."

"I'll take your word for it," said Ron, helping himself to black pudding.[1]

LEARNING FROM THE PAST

You may also find some deeper and heavier discussions coming out of *Harry Potter and the Goblet of Fire*. My son connected the Death Eaters and the dark mark with slavery and the Holocaust. It gave us an excellent opportunity to discuss what can happen when people are intolerant of different cultures.

While at the Quidditch World Cup, a group of individuals don hooded robes and masks to hide their identity, levitate a Muggle family into the air and parade them through the crowd. The family is treated with disrespect. The behavior of the robed persons shows intolerance for differences in others and represents an attempt to establish power and superiority over others who are different. Use the scenes from chapter nine to discuss real tragedies that have resulted because of intolerance.

QUESTIONS TO BRIDGE THE GAP

- **Why would these wizards cloak themselves and act like that? Why do others join in? What are the results of their actions?**

- **When have similar events really happened?**

- **What causes people to treat others so violently?**

- **How can such abuse and violence be prevented? What can you do?**

- **When have you seen others treated disrespectfully because of their differences? What did you do? What should you do?**

I suggest that such discussions are most appropriate for children who are in the sixth grade and older. But all children mature differently. Some younger children may already have learned about slavery, groups like the Ku Klux Klan and the Holocaust. You can adjust the discussion accordingly.

SIGNS OF HATE

Sometimes signs and symbols are also used to spread fear and hate. In *Harry Potter and the Goblet of Fire* we also learn about the "dark mark" and how Voldemort has used it to spread hate, fear and discord and to organize his followers. A further explanation of the dark mark can be found in chapter nine of *Harry Potter and the Goblet of Fire*.

BEARING WITNESS WITH RESPECT

Faith will inevitably work its way into discussions about cultural diversity. As my children talked about the different customs and cultures of their classmates and friends, they also mentioned some of the different religious beliefs and customs of other children. They were perplexed by one child's belief that each person has his or her own individual God and another child's assertion that she didn't believe in God.

QUESTIONS TO BRIDGE THE GAP

- **What signs and symbols have been used in the past to spread hate and fear?**

- **How do gangs use signs and symbols? How do those symbols make you feel?**

- **What can you do when you become aware of a sign or symbol that is being used to spread fear and hate?**

- **What signs and symbols are used to spread love and harmony?**

I asked my children how they responded to these friends. I was happy to hear that they respected these differing opinions and beliefs but had also told their friends that they believe in one God who created all of us.

When religious topics come up in conversations with peers, children, like adults, can take advantage of these discussions to talk about their own faith. While we must respect others' beliefs, we Christians are called to speak about and stand by our faith in Christ. Diversity discussions growing out of Harry Potter reading may allow you to empower your children to communicate their faith to others. In a discussion about religious beliefs children can share their faith by asking, "Would you like me to tell you about Jesus?" or "Have you ever read the Bible? Do you know what it says about God and Jesus?"

11

HIDING HURTS

It was costing him every bit of determination he had to keep talking,
yet he sensed that once he finished, he would feel better.

HARRY POTTER AND THE GOBLET OF FIRE

As you discuss the Harry Potter stories with children, you are likely to uncover emotions and pain that have been repressed. Children who have experienced trauma often hide their pain and anger. Anger and hostility can also build up in response to everyday stresses that have not been particularly traumatic. In our fallen human nature, we usually bury these feelings. However, burying them does not make them go away.

Discussing these issues will bring many past hurts to the surface. In fact, you will likely find your own past hurts surfacing. This is healthy and necessary.

In *The Whole Child*, philosopher and child psychologist Seamus Carey urges parents to face their own repressed pains and hurts. He has found that when parents repress their hurts and needs, they subconsciously try to meet their needs through their children and ultimately end up neglecting their children's needs. He argues that we cannot truly meet the needs of others until we have worked through our pain and hurt.[1] Thus we need to uncover our own past hurts and heal.

QUESTIONS TO BRIDGE THE GAP

- **Sometimes Harry hides his fear and pain. He doesn't let Ron and Hermione know how he is feeling. What keeps him from sharing his fears and pain with his friends?**

- **What pain and fears do you keep inside? What keeps you from letting others know about them?**

- **Why is it important to let some other people know about your feelings and fears?**

- **Who is someone you can trust to listen and guide you?**

It will be up to you to decide whether your experiences are appropriate to recount to your children. If it seems too difficult for a child to understand, it probably is. It will be most appropriate for you to turn to a friend, spouse, pastor or counselor for helping you to work through painful memories.

As you work through your own and others' emotions and pain, listening will be crucial. Carey offers suggestions for effective listening. In quick summary, here are the techniques he recommends:

- Repeat what your child tells you or describe what your child seems to be feeling.

- Concentrate on one feeling or idea.

- Let go of your own thoughts, judgments, fears, inhibitions and prejudices. Hear only your child's words and emotions.[2]

THE POWER OF PRAYER

Another important element of healing comes from God. As we turn to God in prayer, we can receive profound spiritual healing. Encourage children to turn to God with their pain, troubles and problems. God offers healing and guidance that even wise human parents cannot provide.

While the magical world of Harry Potter is fun to explore with children and may bring us back to reality refreshed, we know that Harry Potter's magical powers are not real. We could wish and wave wooden sticks in hopes that our problems would disappear, but we know that only God has healing and saving powers. God's power is real, and he shares it with us freely. All we need to do is ask. For Jesus tells us: "Ask and you will receive; seek and you will find; knock and the door will be opened to you. For everyone who asks, receives; and the one who seeks, finds; and to the one who knocks, the door will be opened" (Luke 11:9-10).

Jesus means this. He wants us to trust God with all of our needs. God hears all prayers and loves to hear from us. He doesn't judge our heartfelt words to him.

Pray from your heart, and your children will learn to do the same. Your children will learn to trust in a powerful God who listens to and answers their prayers. In a society that promises power based on worldly possessions and control of others, we must teach children to rely on God. As we talk to them about the power of prayer, we introduce them to a God who cares about and listens to all of their pain, troubles and fears. We teach them to trust in a God who rejoices in their victories. They learn to trust in a God who forgives them no matter what and loves them deeply and unconditionally.

QUESTIONS TO BRIDGE THE GAP

- **How would Harry's life be different if he learned to trust in God?**

- **Harry often relies on magic to solve his problems. We don't have magic. We have something more powerful: we have a God who knows and loves us. How can prayer help us in times of trouble?**

- **How is prayer different from magic?**

- **How would Harry be different if he believed and trusted in God?**

12

Letting Go of Anger

*Every bitter and resentful thought that Harry
had had in the past month was pouring out of him.*

As you listen to children who have experienced profound pain,
you will likely find that they are full of anger and rage. Children often
need help in working through anger. Not surprisingly, the Harry Potter books portray many characters who also experience anger.

In fact, Harry is angry throughout most of *Harry Potter and the Order of the Phoenix*. We don't blame him. We get angry with him as he
faces being expelled for merely defending himself, repeatedly suffers
unfair detentions, is forbidden from playing Quidditch and sees his
best friends made prefects. Unfortunately, he often represses his anger rather than talking through it and releasing it. This isolates him
from his friends and fuels hostility.

One day Hermione and Ron try to reach out to Harry. Instead of
taking the opportunity to talk through his angry emotions, Harry
lashes out.

> "Anyway, what's up, Harry?" Hermione continued . . . "You look
> really angry about something."

"Seamus reckons Harry's lying about You-Know-Who," said Ron succinctly, when Harry did not respond.

Hermione, whom Harry had expected to react angrily on his behalf, sighed.

"Yes, Lavender thinks so too," she said gloomily.

"Been having a nice little chat with her about whether or not I'm a lying, attention-seeking prat, have you?" Harry said loudly.

"No," said Hermione calmly, "I told her to keep her big fat mouth shut about you, actually. And it would be quite nice if you stopped jumping down Ron's and my throats, Harry, because if you haven't noticed, we're on your side."[1]

Anger is a part of life. Watching others deal with anger appropriately or inappropriately provides a context for helping us understand how we deal with anger. Here Harry deals with it inappropriately: he represses his feelings and lashes out at his friends. Fortunately, Ron and Hermione don't abandon him. As good friends, they stick by him and remind him that they are there to help and support him. Hermione stays calm even under attack and wisely responds, "We're on your side." Later in the scene, she shows even more wisdom as she reminds Ron and Harry what Dumbledore had said at the end-of-term feast the previous year: "About You-Know-Who. He said, 'His gift for spreading discord and enmity is very great. We can fight it only by showing an equally strong bond of friendship and trust.'"[2]

Hermione provides us with a wonderful example of how to communicate with angry children. We assure them that we are on their side. We help them trust and confide in us. And we remind them that, like Voldemort, Satan feeds on anger. He wants us to be angry with one another. To fight him and to find peace and happiness, we need to stick together in friendship and love. Getting stuck in anger brings only discord, hostility, violence, pain and suffering.

The Harry Potter stories provide us with opportunities to demonstrate healthy ways of working through anger. As you encounter situations in which characters act out of anger and rage, discuss the following:

- Who is angry?

- What is causing the anger?

- How is that character responding to the anger?

- What is happening because of the expression of anger? Is it positive or negative?

- How could the character release his or her anger more effectively?

Barbara Coloroso tells us that our children need "to know it is all right to feel. Feelings are not good or bad per se. It's what your child does with his feelings that makes all the difference. Feelings are motivators for growth or warning signs that something needs to change. He needs to mourn any loss, be it loss of security, belongings, sense of well-being, academic progress, or social interactions. . . . To heal and move on, he must be able to tell his story and be believed, have his pain acknowledged and his anger expressed."[3]

SUGGESTIONS FOR DEALING WITH ANGER

- Breathe deeply and count to ten. Imagine yourself releasing your anger with each number and breath.

- Blow up a balloon. Imagine yourself blowing all of your anger into the balloon. After it is blown up, release the balloon and watch all the anger float away.

- Go outdoors and blow bubbles. Blow your anger into the bubbles and watch them float away.

- Pound a pillow or your bed.

- Go down to the basement or outdoors and yell loudly.

- Draw a picture or write in a journal. Let all of your feelings out on paper.

- Play with toy figures in a tub, bucket or sink of water.

- Play with clay or Play-Doh. Release your anger and tension into the clay.

- Go outside. Run, exercise, play catch, shoot hoops or swing.

All these practices are healthy ways to release the anger. By encouraging children to release anger, you help them avoid hurting themselves or others.

13

GETTING HELP

What he really wanted (and it felt almost shameful to admit it to himself) was someone like—someone like a parent: an adult wizard whose advice he could ask without feeling stupid, someone who cared about him.

HARRY POTTER AND THE GOBLET OF FIRE

Like anyone else, children sometimes suffer. A mishap may cause minor bumps and bruises, or they may find themselves in serious danger. It is important that during such times they know whom to turn to for help. Like adults, however, they may be hindered by pride and fear. Asking for help seems like admitting weakness, and others may have betrayed them when they confided a painful secret. Adults in authority sometimes use their power and position to abuse children. Children need help in discerning when and whom to trust.

Harry faces many problems and has a lot of repressed pain and emotions to work out. He struggles with trust because he is often abused by his guardians, the Dursleys. Many children reading these books will be working through similar situations. Talking about Harry's situations and decisions will make it easier for children to open up about their own struggles. It also gives us a chance to offer guidance on whom to trust and when. Not only may these discussions reveal and stop present hurts and traumas, but they can help children decide what to do when future problems arise.

At one point in *Harry Potter and the Chamber of Secrets,* Dumbledore intuitively knows that something is bothering Harry and asks Harry if there's anything that he'd like to tell him about.

QUESTIONS TO BRIDGE THE GAP

- **When was the last time someone offered to help you and you turned them down? What kept you from accepting the help?**

- **How can you overcome your pride and accept God's loving help?**

- **"Man's pride causes his humiliation, but he who is humble of spirit obtains honor" (Proverbs 29:23). How is this Scripture passage reflected in Harry's behavior?**

- **How is it reflected in your life?**

Harry didn't know what to say. He thought of Malfoy shouting, "You'll be next, Mudbloods!" and of the Polyjuice potion simmering away in Moaning Myrtle's bathroom. Then he thought of the disembodied voice he had heard twice and remembered what Ron had said: *"Hearing voices no one else can hear isn't a good sign, even in the wizarding world."* He thought, too, about what everyone was saying about him, and his growing dread that he was somehow connected with Salazar Slytherin. . . .

"No," said Harry. "There isn't anything, Professor."[1]

Harry could have received help from a trusted adult and felt much better, but his pride gets in the way. Sometimes we act as Harry does here: instead of getting help, we hide our fears and problems. God often sends help our way, but our pride may keep us from accepting it.

WHOM TO TRUST?

I have learned much from conversations with my children, based on Harry Potter discussions.

It is not always easy to seek out help from others or even to accept help if it's offered. Fear and pride often hold us back. Sometimes we can figure things out on our own, but most often it is wise to turn to a trusted adult for help. The key is to let go of our fear and take that first step to get help. We also need to know whom we can trust.

God often sends special people into our lives who know just how to help us. They have the right words to say at the right time, and they know how to lead us to the help we need. To find these people, we need to pray and open our hearts and minds to God.

Trust does not and should not come easily. It is not wise to confide in everyone we meet. Trust comes with time. It is earned by repeated examples of care and concern. Parents and guardians earn trust by caring for our daily needs. We can feel their care and concern. We grow to feel God's love through them. They strive for what is right, and they fight against what is evil. They listen to us and care about our thoughts and feelings. They don't physically or verbally harm us. They don't ask us to lie or keep secrets that may harm us or others. While they may make mistakes that hurt our feelings from time to time, they always show remorse, ask forgiveness and avoid the mistake in the future. We earn the trust of others by doing the same.

Trusted adults may be parents and guardians, family members, friends, ministers, doctors, teachers, counselors and so on. But just being part of our family or having authority does not make an adult trustworthy. For example, the Dursleys are members of Harry's family and his guardians, but they abuse him; he certainly must not trust them. People in any of these roles can prove to be untrustworthy.

Trust must be earned. Prayer and discernment helps us to know whom to trust.

Abuse comes in many forms, and children need to learn whom to trust and when. Discussing various situations and individuals common to your lives will help your children figure out to whom they could turn for help in times of trouble.

In *Harry Potter and the Prisoner of Azkaban,* Harry takes the risk of trusting Professor Lupin with his troubles, and in turn Professor Lupin helps Harry understand his fears.

> "I didn't think of Voldemort," said Harry honestly. "I—I remembered those dementors."
>
> "I see," said Lupin thoughtfully. "Well, well . . . I'm impressed." He smiled slightly at the look of surprise on Harry's face. "That suggests that what you fear most of all is— fear. Very wise, Harry."[2]

Later Harry goes a little further and takes a bigger risk. Professor Lupin has proven trust-

QUESTIONS TO BRIDGE THE GAP

- Harry's greatest fear is fear. Lupin finds this wise. Do you? Why or why not?

- What is your greatest fear? How do you deal with that fear?

- How could you turn that fear over to God?

- "Do not fear. . . . Do not turn to meaningless idols which can neither profit nor save; they are nothing. For the sake of his own great name the LORD will not abandon his people. . . . But you must fear the LORD and worship him faithfully with your whole heart; keep in mind the great things he has done among you" (1 Samuel 12:20-24). What does this Scripture passage from 1 Samuel teach us about fear?

- How could this passage help Harry?

- How can you apply it to your life?

worthy by warding off a dementor on the train and helping Harry understand his fears. He has shown sincere concern and compassion. So Harry decides to turn to the professor for more help. He confides his fears and questions regarding the dementors and asks Professor Lupin to help him find a way to fight them off. Professor Lupin teaches him how to battle the dementors and practices with him regularly.

QUESTIONS TO BRIDGE THE GAP

- How does Professor Lupin show that he can be trusted?

- How does he respond to what Harry reveals?

- Why is it hard for Harry to confess his feelings to Professor Lupin?

- When have you talked to someone about your personal feelings? How did you feel while you were sharing? How did you feel afterward?

- Was it wise for Harry to trust Professor Lupin? Why?

- What are some things for which you might need to get help from an adult? Why?

- Whom can you trust when you need help? How has this person earned your trust?

- Who are some people you *shouldn't* trust for help? Why?

Harry shows great courage as he opens up to Lupin. He swallows his pride, though he wonders if his reaction to the dementors signifies weakness. Professor Lupin senses this before Harry even asks, but assures him that is not the case. In the end, Harry is successful in learning to ward off the dementors. Professor Lupin has taught him how to protect himself. Harry saves his own life, as well as Sirius's and Hermione's because of his courageous decision to seek out help.[3]

14

Choosing Good over Evil

*It was the last thing they wanted to do,
but what choice did they have?*

Harry Potter and the Sorcerer's Stone

✳

It is not difficult to spot the Christian parallels and themes that run through the Harry Potter series. The most obvious of these is the battle of good against evil.

Lord Voldemort and Satan share many characteristics. Voldemort seeks power and immortality. He has the power to possess bodies and inhabit snakes. He has an evil group of followers called the Death Eaters, who hate and kill "Mudbloods" (wizards who were not born from wizards—Hermione is an example) and anyone who stands in their way. Yet good always triumphs over evil, and Harry defeats Voldemort. Love, moral character and sacrifice are essential components in the defeat.

Satan is the father of all lies. Like Voldemort, he uses humans' greed for power and money to attract followers. Draco Malfoy and his father, loyal followers under Voldermort's spell, are perfect examples of this. Satan lives to bring suffering and death to all of us. Like Harry, we are in the midst of a constant battle of good versus evil. And like Harry, we need to remain strong, alert and principled. We can easily

QUESTIONS TO BRIDGE THE GAP

- **Why is love so much more powerful than hate?**

- **When have you acted out of hate? What happened? How could you have acted out of love? How would the outcome have been different?**

be led astray by Satan's lies, but as we learn Scripture and follow Christ's teachings, not witchcraft, we can win our battle against Satan. As Paul tells us in Ephesians 6:11, we must "put on the armor of God so that [we] may be able to stand firm against the tactics of the devil."

In *Harry Potter and the Chamber of Secrets,* Harry discovers that he has qualities of his parents, yet he also has some of Voldemort's talents and powers. He wonders whether he is destined to be evil like Voldemort. Like all humans, he has potential for both good and evil. But Dumbledore explains, "It is our choices, Harry, that show what we truly are, far more than our abilities." This reinforces biblical teachings: God has given us free will to choose whether to do good or to do evil. Harry experiences the same struggle that we do, and sometimes he makes poor choices—like breaking school rules—that bring negative consequences. But in the end, he chooses good, not evil. Good triumphs. We also must choose good over evil. As we choose to follow the teachings of Christ, we can avoid the deceptions and evils of Satan.

GOD IN THE HARRY POTTER TALES

None of the characters in the books is an adequate parallel to God or Jesus. Be sure that your children do not see Harry Potter as a Godlike figure. Harry is a closer parallel to us: he struggles as we do. Children may also be tempted to see Dumbledore as a parallel for God. But Dumbledore is not God; he is more like a prophet. Dumbledore helps

Harry make sense of the battle and gives him advice and knowledge.

He helps Harry understand that he is alive because his mother died to save him. Her love protects him.

Be sure to note that the love of Harry's mother saves Harry, not Harry's mother herself. If you don't make this distinction, your children may equate Harry's mother with Christ. It is love that saves Harry, and God is love. Just as Dumbledore often explains things for Harry, the apostle Paul helps us understand this concept: "God proves his love for us in that while we were still sinners Christ died for us. How much more then, since we are now justified by his blood, will we be saved through him from the wrath" (Romans 5:8-9).

No fictional character could

QUESTIONS TO BRIDGE THE GAP

- While being sorted, Harry is told that he can be great if he chooses Slytherin. Harry is tempted, but in the end he chooses Gryffindor. Why do you think Harry is sorted into Gryffindor? Why doesn't he want to be sorted into Slytherin?

- When have you been tempted to do something against God's teachings? Why was it tempting? What did you do?

- Sometimes we don't make the Christian choice. We are led astray by money, friends or things. What can we do to receive forgiveness and get back on track?

- How can we avoid these temptations?

or should adequately represent God. We learn about God in Scripture. But we can and should apply scriptural teachings to all that enters our minds and hearts. Thus, by connecting the themes of good and evil in the Harry Potter books with the teachings of Christ and the responsibilities that go with being a Christian, we can help children to connect all aspects of their lives to Christ.

HARRY MEETS JESUS

The best way to incorporate God into your Harry Potter discussions is by turning to Scripture. Harry has not yet found God. Ask your children what Jesus teaches about the various situations you encounter in the stories. What would Jesus do? What advice would you give Harry? Why is Jesus' power much greater than that of witchcraft? Why does God abhor witchcraft?

Jesus performed miracles. He turned water to wine, healed the sick, made the blind see, brought the dead to life and rose from death himself. God is our powerful protector. It is important that children do not confuse a real and powerful God with a magical, fictional character. Jesus was real; Harry Potter is imaginary. Miracles are a wonderful reality of our faith; magic is fictional and against the teachings of our faith. Most children brought up in the church already understand this, but it is still good to do a reality check from time to time. For example, when I led the Bible Adventure station one summer at vacation Bible school, I asked the children how the Bible differed from other books like the Harry Potter stories. Without hesitation, they all yelled out: "The Bible is true! The stories there really happened!"

You can reinforce children's love of and trust in God while you enjoy the imaginary tales of Harry Potter. As your children marvel at the fantasy world and battles, discuss questions like: How could Jesus have helped Harry? What would you tell Harry about Jesus? How does Jesus help you with your battles at school? Or say something like "This is a fun story, but magic isn't real. Satan likes to trick us and make us think we can have magical powers, like the way Voldemort tricked Ginny with the diary of Tom Riddle. But Jesus taught us to trust in God and take our problems to him. God loves us, and Jesus died to save us. Only God has the power to save us."

Some children will make these connections on their own. While reading the books with my children, I was amazed at how they connected the story with their faith. As we read *Harry Potter and the Chamber of Secrets,* my son Adam compared Harry's plunging the basilisk fang into Tom Riddle's diary and destroying it to Christ's destroying Satan's book of lies when soldiers drove nails into Christ's hands and feet. Despite that violence, he noted, Christ later rose from the dead. Further, the way the Phoenix tears heal Harry's wound is similar to the way Christ's tears and suffering heal our wounds. The Phoenix rises out of the ashes and saves Harry, as Christ rose from the dead to save us. Adam was only in fourth grade when he noticed these parallels.

Children's imaginations and open minds allow them to form powerful connections that will not only strengthen their faith but help us as well. My children commonly speak in metaphors that help me see the world in a new way. Sometimes we need to step back and see the world and our faith afresh through the eyes of our children. Paul tells the Romans: "For as in one body we have many parts, and all the parts do not have the same function, so we, though many, are one body in Christ and individually parts of one another. Since we have gifts that differ according to the grace given to us, let us exercise them" (Romans 12:4-7). Our children, too, are members of the body of Christ, and we can learn from them.

15

THE POWER OF LOVE

*To have been loved so deeply, even though the person who
loved us is gone, will give us some protection forever.*

PROFESSOR DUMBLEDORE, *HARRY POTTER
AND THE CHAMBER OF SECRETS*

The theme of love dominates all of the Harry Potter books. Love is the reason Harry Potter remains alive and continually defeats Lord Voldemort. Dumbledore reminds us of this at the end of each book. Likewise, love protects and saves each of us. Jesus died to give us the gifts of forgiveness and eternal life. Jesus' love lives in each of us.

Love lives in the core of our being. It gives breath to our soul and helps us in the midst of all our struggles. We know this, but sometimes we forget just how powerful love is. And love can be difficult to discuss with children because of its abstractness. The Harry Potter stories give us much-needed opportunities to discuss

QUESTIONS TO BRIDGE THE GAP

- How are you marked with Jesus' love?

- How does love protect you?

- When have you felt love?

- How do you show love to others?

- Why is love more powerful than magic?

- How did Jesus' love save you?

the power of love. Children begin to understand love's power as it protects Harry from Voldemort. It is love that protects Harry, not magic. The stories become teaching tools to help children understand how Jesus' love protects us from sin and death.

In *Harry Potter and the Sorcerer's Stone* we learn that Harry's mother's love "left its own mark" and saved him.[1] Voldemort does not understand love and cannot stand to touch a person "marked by something so good."[2]

EVERLASTING

The Harry Potter books also remind us that love reaches beyond the graves of our loved ones. This offers reassurance to children who are grieving loved ones—as well as adults. Reading and discussing these books help children to open up and talk about death. Harry has lost his parents, yet he still feels their love. In fact, in *Harry Potter and the Prisoner of Azkaban* when he wonders why his Patronus takes on the shape of a stag, his father's "animagus," Dumbledore questions:

QUESTIONS TO BRIDGE THE GAP

- **How does Harry feel about being without his parents?**

- **When have you lost someone you loved? How did you feel?**

- **How does Harry feel his parents' love even though they are not with him?**

- **How and when do you feel the love of your loved ones who have died?**

- **Why did Harry's Patronus take the same shape of his father's animagus?**

- **How do you remember your loved ones who have died? How do they help you in times of trouble? How do they live on in you?**

- **How do you feel Jesus' love?**

- **How do you call on Jesus' love in times of trouble?**

- **How does Jesus' love live on through you? How do you share his love with others?**

"You think the dead we loved ever truly leave us? You think that we don't recall them more clearly than ever in times of great trouble? Your father is alive in you, Harry, and shows himself most plainly when you have need of him. How else could you produce that *particular* Patronus? Prongs rode again last night. . . . You found him inside yourself."[3]

16

FACING SPIRITUAL BATTLES

We are all facing dark and difficult times.

PROFESSOR DUMBLEDORE,
HARRY POTTER AND THE GOBLET OF FIRE

Each day we choose between good and evil, although we may not notice that we're doing so. When we act out of love, we choose good, and when we act out of hate, we choose evil. We quickly know which side we aligned ourselves with when we face the consequences of our actions.

Throughout the Harry Potter books our children are reminded of the opposing forces of good and evil. Harry struggles with his choices on a daily basis, just as we do. Sometimes he makes mistakes and must face the consequences of his actions, but many times he makes good choices and defeats evil with love. Love is something that Voldemort does not possess, and it is much more powerful than hatred and magic.

Satan does not know love, and thus Jesus defeated Satan with his loving sacrifice for us. We too defeat Satan when we reach out and love others. This is our spiritual battle. In choosing to love, we defeat Satan and his evil.

RECOGNIZING OUR ABILITIES

Sometimes we forget how powerful love is, and we underestimate our abilities to fight evil in the world. We get tired and frustrated with the battle against evil. We can relate to Harry at the end of *Harry Potter and the Order of the Phoenix* when he worries about future battles with Voldemort. He forgets his own abilities as he tells Dumbledore, "I haven't any powers he hasn't got, I couldn't fight the way he did tonight, I can't possess people or—or kill them."[1] We also doubt our abilities and get frustrated with our imperfections as we strive to be like Jesus. But Dumbledore reminds Harry that he has one power that Voldemort will never have—love!

QUESTIONS TO BRIDGE THE GAP

- **When have you chosen good over evil? What happened?**

- **When have you chosen evil over good? What happened?**

- **What is the force that Voldemort and Satan detest?**

- **How can Harry use that force to his advantage? How has he used it thus far?**

- **How do you use that force in your Christian battle against sin and Satan?**

- **Why is love more powerful than hate?**

- **How can you help others find this force in their hearts and use it for good?**

NOTES

Chapter 1: The Harry Hype
[1]Elizabeth Shafer, *Exploring Harry Potter* (Osprey, Fla.: Beacham, 2000), p. 32.

[2]Ibid., p. 30.

[3]"The Truth About Harry Potter," <http://www.freedomvillageusa.com/ABC2.htm> (accessed October 1, 2002).

[4]"Where Has Harry Potter Been Banned?" Muggles for Harry Potter, <http://www.muggles-forharrypotter.org> (accessed October 1, 2000).

[5]Elizabeth Gleick, "Book Banning Hits a Road Block: The First Amendment," *Time*, October 2000, <http://www.time.com/time/daily/),2980,33449,00.html> (accessed October 1, 2000).

[6]Carol Hurst, "Believing in Children as Readers, Learners and Teachers," <http://www.carol-hurst.com/profsubjects/reading/believing.html> (accessed October 1, 2000).

[7]C. S. Lewis, *The Lion, the Witch and the Wardrobe* (New York: HarperTrophy, 1978), p. 163.

[8]J. K. Rowling, *Harry Potter and the Sorcerer's Stone* (New York: Scholastic, 1997), p. 299.

Chapter 2: More Than a Story
[1]Claudia Royal, *Storytelling: An Ancient Art* (Nashville: Broadman, 1955), p. 24.

[2]Ibid., p. 22.

[3]Robert Coles, *How to Raise a Moral Child: The Moral Intelligence of Children* (New York: Random House, 1997), p. 10.

[4]William Kilpatrick, Suzanne Wolfe and Gregory Wolfe, *Books That Build Character: A Guide to Teaching Your Child Moral Values Through Stories* (New York: Simon & Schuster, 1994), pp. 46-47.

[5]Ibid., p. 47.

[6]William Bennett, *The Book of Virtues* (New York: Simon & Schuster, 1993), p. 13.

Chapter 3: The Modern Fairy Tale
[1]Bruno Bettelheim, *The Uses of Enchantment: The Meaning and Importance of Fairy Tales* (New York: Vintage, 1977), p. 117.

[2]Ibid., p. 4.

[3]Ibid., p. 6.

[4]Ibid., p. 5.

[5]Donald Baker, *Functions of Folk and Fairy Tales* (Washington, D.C.: Association for Childhood Education International, 1981), p. 5.

[6]Max Luthi, *Once upon a Time: On the Nature of Fairy Tales* (Bloomington: Indiana University Press, 1970), p. 139.

[7]J. K. Rowling, *Harry Potter and the Chamber of Secrets* (New York: Scholastic, 1999), p. 276.

[8]Ibid., p. 279.

[9]Bettelheim, *Uses of Enchantment*, p. 8.

[10]Ibid., p. 9.

[11]J. K. Rowling, *Harry Potter and the Sorcerer's Stone* (New York: Scholastic, 1997), p. 59.

[12]Ibid.

Chapter 4: Discussing Fantasy with Children

[1]Donald Baker, *Functions of Folk and Fairy Tales* (Washington, D.C.: Association for Childhood Education International, 1981), p. 8.

[2]Bruno Bettelheim, *The Uses of Enchantment: The Meaning and Importance of Fairy Tales* (New York: Vintage, 1977), p. 7.

[3]Ibid.

[4]Ibid.

[5]Rosemary Haughton, *Tales from Eternity: The World of Fairytales and the Spiritual Search* (New York: Seabury, 1973), p. 18.

[6]Baker, *Functions*, p. 10.

[7]Jack Zipes, *Sticks and Stones: The Troublesome Success of Children's Literature from Slovenly Peter to Harry Potter* (New York: Routledge, 2002), p. 174.

[8]J. K. Rowling, *Harry Potter and the Order of the Phoenix* (New York: Scholastic, 2003), p. 836.

[9]Ibid., p. 844.

[10]Vigen Guroian, *Tending the Heart of Virtue: How Classic Stories Awaken a Child's Moral Imagination* (New York: Oxford University Press, 1998), p. 26.

[11]Ibid., p. 37.

[12]Francis Bridger, *A Charmed Life: The Spirituality of Potterworld* (New York: Doubleday, 2002), p. 31.

[13]J. K. Rowling, *Harry Potter and the Prisoner of Azkaban* (New York: Scholastic, 1999), p. 109.

[14]Ibid, p. 105.

[15]Zipes, *Sticks and Stones,* p. 177.

[16]Perry Nodelman and Mavis Reimer, *The Pleasures of Children's Literature* (Boston: Allyn and Bacon, 2003), p. 313.

Chapter 5: Morals, Not Magic

[1]J. K. Rowling, *Harry Potter and the Chamber of Secrets* (New York: Scholastic, 1999), p. 112.

[2]Ibid., pp. 115-16.

[3]Ronald Duska and Mariellen Whelan, *Moral Development: A Guide to Piaget and Kohlberg* (New York: Paulist, 1975), p. 52.

[4]Jean Piaget, *The Moral Development of the Child* (New York: Free Press, 1965), p. 111; Lawrence Kolhberg, "Continuities and Discontinuities in Childhood and Moral Development," in *Moral Education: Interdisciplinary Approaches* (New York: Newman, 1975), p. 87.

[5]Duska and Whelan, *Moral Development*, p. 76.

[6]Nancy Eisenberg, "Self-Attributions, Social Interaction and Moral Development," in *Moral Development Through Social Interaction,* ed. William M. Kurtines and Jacob L. Gewirtz (New York: John Wiley & Sons, 1987), p. 24.

[7]Ibid.

[8]Duska and Whelan, *Moral Development,* p. 52.

[9]R. S. Peters. *Moral Development and Moral Education* (London: George Allen & Unwin, 1981), p. 174.

[10]Lawrence J. Walker et al., "Reasoning About Morality and Real-Life Moral Problems," in *Morality in Everyday Life: Developmental Perspectives,* ed. Melanie Killen and Daniel Hart (New York: Cambridge University Press, 1995), p. 372.
[11]J. K. Rowling, *Harry Potter and the Sorcerer's Stone* (New York: Scholastic, 1997), p. 137.

Chapter 6: The Real Issues in Harry Potter
[1]Perry Nodelman and Mavis Reimer, *The Pleasures of Children's Literature* (Boston: Allyn and Bacon, 2003), p. 37.
[2]Ibid., pp. 35-36.

Chapter 7: Dealing with Traumatic Experiences
[1]J. K. Rowling, *Harry Potter and the Goblet of Fire* (New York: Scholastic, 2000), pp. 18-19.
[2]Duncan B. Clark and Thomas W. Miller. "Stress Response and Adaptation in Children: Theoretical Models," in *Children of Trauma,* ed. Thomas W. Miller (Madison, Conn.: International Universities Press, 1998), p. 8.
[3]Michael Schulman and Eva Mekler, *Bringing Up a Moral Child* (New York: Doubleday, 1994), p. 152.

Chapter 9: Battling Bullies
[1]Barbara Coloroso, *The Bully, the Bullied and the Bystander* (New York: HarperResource, 2003), p. 149.
[2]Ibid., p. 149.
[3]J. K. Rowling, *Harry Potter and the Order of the Phoenix* (New York: Scholastic, 2003), p. 412.
[4]Ibid., p. 413.

Chapter 10: Delving into Diversity
[1]J. K. Rowling, *Harry Potter and the Goblet of Fire* (New York: Scholastic, 2000), p. 251.

Chapter 11: Hiding Hurts
[1]Seamus Carey, *The Whole Child* (Lanham, Md.: Rowman & Littlefield, 2003), p. 56.
[2]Ibid., pp. 72-74.

Chapter 12: Letting Go of Anger
[1]J. K. Rowling, *Harry Potter and the Order of the Phoenix* (New York: Scholastic, 2003), pp. 222-23.
[2]Ibid., p. 223.
[3]Barbara Coloroso, *The Bully, the Bullied and the Bystander* (New York: HarperResource, 2003), p. 153.

Chapter 13: Getting Help
[1]J. K. Rowling, *Harry Potter and the Chamber of Secrets* (New York: Scholastic, 1999), pp. 208-9.
[2]J. K. Rowling, *Harry Potter and the Prisoner of Azkaban* (New York: Scholastic, 1999), p. 155.
[3]Ibid., p. 188.

Chapter 15: The Power of Love
[1]J. K. Rowling, *Harry Potter and the Sorcerer's Stone* (New York: Scholastic, 1999), p. 299.

[2]Ibid.

[3]J. K. Rowling, *Harry Potter and the Prisoner of Azkaban* (New York: Scholastic, 1999), pp. 427-28.

Chapter 16: Facing Spiritual Battles

[1]J. K. Rowling, *Harry Potter and the Order of the Phoenix* (New York: Scholastic, 2003), p. 843.